Credits

Author
Adam Boduch

Reviewers
Md. Mahmud Ahsan
Nick Gajewski
Shameemah Kurzawa
Joe Wu

Acquisition Editor
Sarah Cullington

Development Editor
Gaurav Mehta

Technical Editors
Gauri Iyer
Pooja Pande Malik

Project Coordinator
Joel Goveya

Proofreader
Aaron Nash

Indexer
Hemangini Bari

Graphics
Nilesh R. Mohite
Valentina J. D'silva

Production Coordinator
Aparna Bhagat

Cover Work
Kruthika Bangera
Aparna Bhagat

About the Author

Adam Boduch has been programming in Python for nearly a decade. He is experienced in working with several web frameworks such as Django and Twisted. He likes to experiment with integrating JavaScript tools such as jQuery UI into these frameworks.

Adam has been working for Enomaly Inc. since 2006. He started working with content management systems before making the transition to ECP, where he designed several user interface components using jQuery UI. He now leads the SpotCloud cloud computing market-place project.

I'd like to thank Melissa and Jason for their endless love and support, without which, this book would not have been possible.

About the Reviewers

Md. **Mahmud Ahsan** graduated in Computer Science & Engineering from the International Islamic University Chittagong (IIUC) in Bangladesh. He is a Zend Certified engineer and has experience of more than six years in LAMP-based web applications development He is an expert in developing APIs and mashup applications in Facebook, LinkedIn, and Twitter. Besides his full-time freelance work, he blogs at `http://thinkdiff.net` and also writes articles in different technologies such as Facebook application development. He lives in Bangladesh with his wife, Jinat.

Currently, he is working as a freelancer, managing and developing social web applications, using technologies such as PHP, MySQL, JavaScript, Zend Framework, CodeIgniter, jQuery, and Mashup APIs. He also leads various small- to medium-level projects.

He is also an Indie iPhone application developer and publishes the applications he develops at `http://ithinkdiff.net`.

He has worked as a technical reviewer on *Zend Framework 1.8 Web Application Development* and *PHP jQuery Cookbook* by Packt Publishing.

> I am very grateful to my father, who bought me a computer in 2001. Since then, I was able to explore my love for programming and work in various technologies.

Nick Gajewski is a user interface and Drupal developer. He lives in Toronto, Ontario, Canada.

Originally tinkering with websites during the years of the Internet Explorer and Netscape browser wars, he took a partial hiatus from the world of the Internet to educate the youth of today.

After five years in the education trenches, he was lured back into web development and design through its innovation, creativity, and limitless possibilities. Now, with four years of experience under his belt, he builds front-end and offers Drupal solutions for Enomaly Inc. and freelances under `nickgajewski.com`.

He enjoys creating websites that are exciting, innovative, and are a pleasure for the users to experience.

I would like to thank my family for their support, encouragement, humor, and delicious Polish food.

Shameemah Kurzawa started programming when she was in high school. Being motivated to be a System Analyst, she pursued both undergraduate and postgraduate studies in Business Information System and Software Engineering, respectively.

She has been working as a Web Developer/Analyst for the past five years at a renowned broadcasting company in Australia, SBS (Special Broadcasting Service). Besides work, she enjoys spending her time with family. She is a mother of a little baby boy, aged two. She also enjoys travelling, cooking, as well as reading about new technologies.

I would like to thank my husband, my son, and the Packt Publishing team for the support and understanding in reviewing this book.

Joe Wu is a full-time Senior PHP Web Developer, and has been in the industry since 2005. He has worked on various projects of all sizes, and is familiar with most of the Open-Source technologies surrounding PHP Web Development.

Joe is always enthusiastic about new and upcoming technologies, and is keen to learn and pick up a new skill-set wherever possible and utilize them in his current or future projects. He is also keen on learning about new opportunities and innovative ideas, and believes that the market is always wide open for new and upcoming innovations to improve our ways of living.

Apart from all the technological computer work, Joe is a professional Badminton Player and manages to fit a near full-time training schedule along with his full-time job. Joe's best ranking of 59th in the world in singles and the attendance of Commonwealth Games Delhi 2010 means that he has equally as much experience in Badminton and Web Developing.

Apart from all the endeavors, Joe also works for his own company (with his business partner) to put his skills and experience to good use and help anyone who needs assistance with web development.

Wackyinnovation (`www.wackyinnovation.com`) promotes the concept of always moving forward and coming up with and utilizing new technologies and ideas. Their always enthusiastic and can-do attitude ensures jobs are done to perfection with an innovative edge to their competitors.

I would like to thank everyone around me for their continued support both towards badminton and work, especially my fiancé who has to put up with my endless endeavors and dreams that I am pursuing.

---

www.PacktPub.com

Support files, eBooks, discount offers and more

You might want to visit www.PacktPub.com for support files and downloads related to your book.

Did you know that Packt offers eBook versions of every book published, with PDF and ePub files available? You can upgrade to the eBook version at www.PacktPub.com and as a print book customer, you are entitled to a discount on the eBook copy. Get in touch with us at service@packtpub.com for more details.

At www.PacktPub.com, you can also read a collection of free technical articles, sign up for a range of free newsletters and receive exclusive discounts and offers on Packt books and eBooks.

http://PacktLib.PacktPub.com

Do you need instant solutions to your IT questions? PacktLib is Packt's online digital book library. Here, you can access, read and search across Packt's entire library of books.

Why Subscribe?

- ◆ Fully searchable across every book published by Packt
- ◆ Copy and paste, print and bookmark content
- ◆ On demand and accessible via web browser

Free Access for Packt account holders

If you have an account with Packt at www.PacktPub.com, you can use this to access PacktLib today and view nine entirely free books. Simply use your login credentials for immediate access.

Table of Contents

Preface

Welcome to *jQuery UI Themes: Beginner's Guide*. This introductory text will get you started with developing your own themes for jQuery UI applications. Starting with the general concepts of user interface themes, this book walks the reader through everything from the most basic ideas in jQuery UI to more advanced topics such as icons and themes for custom widgets.

What this book covers

Chapter 1, Themeable User Interfaces, talks about themes in general and why they're important for user interfaces. We'll also address some introductory jQuery UI theme concepts.

Chapter 2, Using Themes, explains how to apply jQuery UI themes by example. Here, we'll walk through some introductory examples that use jQuery UI themes.

Chapter 3, Using the ThemeRoller, introduces the ThemeRoller application. This chapter walks the reader through all available ThemeRoller settings and shows how to download and use your theme.

Chapter 4, Working with Widget Containers, explains how to theme widget containers. Containers are the basic building block for themes and this chapter explains a little theory and gives plenty of examples.

Chapter 5, Transforming Interaction States, talks about the different states jQuery UI widgets go through. These states have different visual appearances and you'll find numerous examples on how to customize them.

Chapter 6, Customizing Interaction Cues, gives examples of using interaction cues with jQuery UI. There is a little theory on what they are, as well as examples on how to theme them.

Chapter 7, Creating Theme Icons, talks about icon sets in jQuery UI themes. We cover how these icons are stored in the image files and how to add your own icons to a theme.

Chapter 8, Special Effects, talks about special effects in the jQuery UI theme framework – rounded corners, and shadows. You'll see several examples of how to apply these classes to widgets and how to customize them.

Chapter 9, Theming Custom Widgets, walks you through the process of constructing a custom widget. We then cover making the widget theme-ready.

What you need for this book

All you need to run the examples in this book are the following:

◆ An Internet connection (for downloading jQuery UI)
◆ A web browser
◆ A text editor
◆ GIMP image editor (free) or PhotoShop (this is required only for chapter 7)

Who this book is for

This book is intended for anyone interested in learning about jQuery UI themes.

Conventions

In this book, you will find several headings appearing frequently.

To give clear instructions of how to complete a procedure or task, we use:

Time for action – heading

Action 1

Action 2

Action 3

Instructions often need some extra explanation so that they make sense, so they are followed with:

What just happened?

This heading explains the working of tasks or instructions that you have just completed.

You will also find some other learning aids in the book, including:

Pop quiz – heading

These are short multiple choice questions intended to help you test your own understanding.

Have a go hero – heading

These set practical challenges and give you ideas for experimenting with what you have learned.

You will also find a number of styles of text that distinguish between different kinds of information. Here are some examples of these styles, and an explanation of their meaning.

Code words in text are shown as follows: "In index.html and index.js, we create three jQuery UI button widgets to show off our new icon."

A block of code is set as follows:

```
$(document).ready(function(){

    $("#my_button").button();

});
```

When we wish to draw your attention to a particular part of a code block, the relevant lines or items are set in bold:

```
#todo-title {
    color: #222222;
    padding-left: 5%;
}

#todo-list {
    font-size: 0.8em;
    color: #362b36;
    list-style-type: square;
}
```

```
h3, ul {

    font-family: Lucida Grande, Lucida Sans, Arial, sans-serif;

}
```

New terms and **important words** are shown in bold. Words that you see on the screen, in menus or dialog boxes for example, appear in the text like this: "If the **Layers** dialog isn't open already, open it by selecting **Windows | Dockable Dialogs | Layers** as illustrated ".

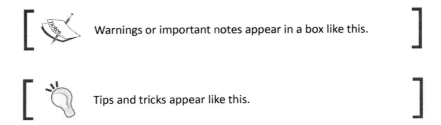

Warnings or important notes appear in a box like this.

Tips and tricks appear like this.

Reader feedback

Feedback from our readers is always welcome. Let us know what you think about this book—what you liked or may have disliked. Reader feedback is important for us to develop titles that you really get the most out of.

To send us general feedback, simply send an e-mail to feedback@packtpub.com, and mention the book title via the subject of your message.

If there is a book that you need and would like to see us publish, please send us a note in the **SUGGEST A TITLE** form on www.packtpub.com or e-mail suggest@packtpub.com.

If there is a topic that you have expertise in and you are interested in either writing or contributing to a book, see our author guide on www.packtpub.com/authors.

Customer support

Now that you are the proud owner of a Packt book, we have a number of things to help you to get the most from your purchase.

Downloading the example code for this book

You can download the example code files for all Packt books you have purchased from your account at http://www.PacktPub.com. If you purchased this book elsewhere, you can visit http://www.PacktPub.com/support and register to have the files e-mailed directly to you.

Errata

Although we have taken every care to ensure the accuracy of our content, mistakes do happen. If you find a mistake in one of our books—maybe a mistake in the text or the code—we would be grateful if you would report this to us. By doing so, you can save other readers from frustration and help us improve subsequent versions of this book. If you find any errata, please report them by visiting http://www.packtpub.com/support, selecting your book, clicking on the **errata submission form** link, and entering the details of your errata. Once your errata are verified, your submission will be accepted and the errata will be uploaded on our website, or added to any list of existing errata, under the Errata section of that title. Any existing errata can be viewed by selecting your title from http://www.packtpub.com/support.

Piracy

Piracy of copyright material on the Internet is an ongoing problem across all media. At Packt, we take the protection of our copyright and licenses very seriously. If you come across any illegal copies of our works, in any form, on the Internet, please provide us with the location address or website name immediately so that we can pursue a remedy.

Please contact us at copyright@packtpub.com with a link to the suspected pirated material.

We appreciate your help in protecting our authors, and our ability to bring you valuable content.

Questions

You can contact us at questions@packtpub.com if you are having a problem with any aspect of the book, and we will do our best to address it.

1

Themeable User Interfaces

Web developers use styles effectively to make web pages look professional. HTML is the structural backbone behind user interfaces viewed on the Web. We can do a lot of interesting things with the look and feel of the Web user experience. We can take an otherwise boring user interface and breathe some life into it.

Giving a web page a look and feel poses the same problem faced by any other software development discipline—how do we prevent ourselves from reinventing the wheel while maintaining usability? We build themeable user interfaces to overcome obstacles such as these.

In this chapter, we will learn the following:

◆ What are themes and widgets and how do they relate?

◆ How to create a basic widget and apply styles to it

◆ Applying basic theming concepts to CSS styles

◆ The basic ideas behind the jQuery UI framework

So let's get on with it.

What is a theme?

Themes represent consistency and familiarity in graphical user interfaces. That is to say, a user interface shouldn't contradict itself by looking vastly different in various contexts. The concept of themes applies to many things humans interact with. This includes both computer user interfaces, as well as those found in the real world.

Themes in the real world

All kinds of real-world things have a theme. Groups of related things share some similarity or another. This also means that they are consistent in some respect. A product line generally has a theme.

A car is a good example of a themed object. Have you ever seen a car in the distance and thought "that is unmistakably Ford"? You don't put a lot of thought into what makes it a Ford, it "just looks like one". This feeling of familiarity is true of different car types. Ford cars and Ford trucks still look like Ford.

This goes beyond the branding that the company logo on the product gives. There are subtleties that give us visual cues that this is a Ford or this is a Mercedes. When either of the companies comes up with a new car, you would instantly know where it came from.

These hidden subtleties that are constant throughout a product line are an example of a theme. Going back to the car example, it is usually the overall shape of the car that give it it's distinctiveness. The small grooves in the body are usually consistent across different models from the manufacture.

The color of a product alone doesn't necessarily dictate the theme in the real world. Seeing the same Subaru wagon in red doesn't hinder our ability to identify the make.

Desktop themes

Your desktop user interface is also themeable. Desktops are made up of windows and other elements within them. The look and feel these elements provide vary with different operating systems. But the function, or the purpose, of say, a button, is universal.

We can change the look and feel of most popular desktop environments by simply changing a preference setting. We can select from a list of available themes that ship with the operating system or we can download a third-party theme someone has created.

We can design desktop themes because there is an API to do this. If a theme author wants to change the border color of all desktop windows, they can do this without changing what a window does. The window looks different but doesn't behave differently.

Themes on the Web

User interfaces built for Web applications don't share the same flexibility as those built for the desktop. There is really no limitation that says we can't build themes that are portable enough to work with more than one application in a web browser. The underlying functionality that gives the desktop applications their look and feel isn't very different from that of a web application.

We can drastically alter the look and feel of a web application with **styles**. Style can be applied to a single HTML element or a range of elements. We have the flexibility to pick and choose which elements we change.

With HTML, there are a variety of ways to achieve the same visual result. For instance, creating portable themes that work across applications. If there was a consistent structure we could apply style to, themes become much simpler to develop, and keep portable. As with the desktop environment, widgets are used in a web environment to make user interfaces themeable.

What are widgets?

Before we start creating our own widgets and styling them, let's take a moment to discuss what widgets actually are. A widget, in the user interface sense, is a portion of anything displayed on the screen. Widgets can be large and complex, or small and simplistic. They usually have at least some structural element that is defined by the developer. A block of text isn't a widget; the developer doesn't specify the shape of each character. Understanding what widgets are and how they relate to themes is important for building themeable user interfaces. For example, the date picker widget solves a common problem—allowing the user to select a date. Themes control how the date picker looks.

Widget structure

Widgets aren't just a single, opaque whole. jQuery UI widgets are structured as assemblies of parts. For instance, below is an equalizer widget. You can see it is made up of several components – the header, and individual sliders for controlling the widget:

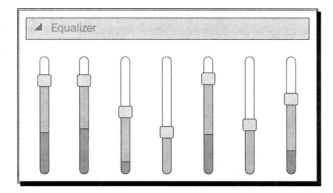

So what are the individual parts that make up a widget? Is there a predefined set of fields that a user interface component must have in order to be considered a widget? There are no qualifying attributes that make something a widget. The fields that define a widget structure are up to the widget creator. They can have a single field and the widget does the rest, or, they can have dozens of fields that allow for a lot of flexibility and are harder to use.

Widgets can contain other widgets. These subordinate widgets can contain others, and so on. We can continue down this path, moving ever further down the ladder until we finally reach the lowest level HTML element. In practice, however, we don't want a complex widget structure that is difficult to style.

Widgets and themes

So how does the structure of a widget, or widgets in general for that matter, relate to themes? Applying a style to a standard HTML element is easy to do. However, in order to share themes, to make them portable, we need to share structure. Theme authors don't design themes for one specific application. They're intended to be used and reused with different applications. The same idea is true for widgets, jQuery UI widgets, Dojo widgets, and so on; they're all intended for reuse.

Portability is an important attribute of widgets. Applying styles to widgets, changing their look and feel, isn't all that different from styling plain old HTML elements. The difference is that the consistency with which the styles are applied to widgets remains the same across applications.

Styling user interfaces

Creating styles that change the look and feel of web application is the reason CSS exists. The many presentation properties that define a style are stored in a style sheet, separate from the structural elements of the user interface. We could directly apply styles to the element as a style attribute. By doing this, we lose all portability; the style is forever bound to the element.

There is more to defining the look and feel of your application when it comes to styling user interfaces. A big part of style creation is structuring your CSS in such a way that they aren't restrictive. Let's take a closer look at what is involved with styling user interfaces.

Time for action - creating a style

Now that we have a general idea of what a widget is and how they relate to themes, let's create one. We're going to create a todo list widget. This widget isn't going to be built for any particular application. We want to reuse it somewhere else, should the need arise. The requirements of this todo list widget are pretty straightforward. It will display the title of the list along with the list items.

1. Create a new `index.html` file with the following content and save it:

```
<html xmlns="http://www.w3.org/1999/xhtml">
    <head>
        <title>Todo List</title>
        <link href="style.css" rel="stylesheet" type="text/css" />
    </head>
    <body>
        <div id="container">
            <h3 id="todo-title">TODO</h3>
            <ul id="todo-list">
                <li>Design user interface</li>
                <li>Implement form validation</li>
                <li>Deploy</li>
            </ul>
        </div>
    </body>
</html>
```

2. In the same directory which has the `index.html` file, create a new `style.css` file and save it:

```
#container {

    background: #f2f5f7;
    border: 3px solid #dddddd;
    width: 25%;
    padding: 3px;

}

#todo-title {

    font-family: Lucida Grande, Lucida Sans, Arial, sans-serif;
    color: #222222;
    padding-left: 5%;

}

#todo-list {
```

```
        font-family: Lucida Grande, Lucida Sans, Arial, sans-serif;
        font-size: 0.8em;
        color: #362b36;
        list-style-type: square;

    }
```

3. Open `index.html` in a web browser. In most operating systems, you should be able to right-click the file and see an option to open the file with the default browser. Alternatively, you can choose **File | Open** to select `index.html`:

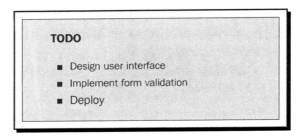

What just happened?

Let's walk through the code and see exactly what we've just created.

The `index.html` file defines the structure of our todo list widget. The `title` element sets the page title to Todo List. The following `link` element imports the CSS file `style.css`. This is where the styles for our todo list widget are defined.

Inside the body tag is the actual todo list widget. The beginning of our widget is the `div` element with the `id` attribute container. Next is the todo list title. The widget title is inside the h3 element with the `id` attribute `todo-title`. Finally, the main purpose of the widget is the list of todo items. The list is the `ul` element with the `id` attribute `todo-list`. Inside the list are all the list items, defined with `li` elements.

The `style.css` file creates the look and feel of our *todo list* widget. There are three styles here that are applied to our widget.

The `#container` style creates a light blue background using the `background` property. The border is displayed as solid gray color using the `border` property. The width is set to 25% of the page using the `width` property. We give the container's contents some additional space with the `padding` property.

The `#todo-title` style sets the font of the todo list title using the `font-family` property. The font color is set to a dark grey using the `color` property. We give a little space to the laft-hand side of the title using the `padding-left` property.

The `#todo-list` style sets the font the same as the `#todo-title` style, using the `font-family` property. The font size is set to be slightly smaller than normal with the `font-size` property. The color is a dark violet and we tell the list to use squares as the bullets.

All these styles are applied to elements by the `id` attribute. This is what the `#` symbol denotes. So the `#container` style applies to the outer `div` element of our todo list.

Style colors

The styles we've just applied to our widget affect the colors of the widget in more ways than one. We set the background, the font, and the border colors of the todo list. You've probably noticed that all colors used are a variant of blue. You might call this style a blue style. The different shades of blue we've chosen complement one another. That is, different border color stands out from the background. It stands out in a complementary way. We could have chosen a different shade of blue that would have been contradictory.

Being able to identify our widget style as "blue" style is a good thing. If our widget had rounded corners, we might identify our style as a "round" style. When we can identify certain traits of a style, we're describing a theme.

This is how the pre-built themes available with jQuery UI are named. The name of each theme describes, as best as it can using a word or two, how the theme looks. For example, the darkness theme uses dark colors while the lightness theme uses light colors. Theme descriptions aren't limited to color shade, they can also describe an analogy in the real-world such as weather, sunny, or overcast. The key idea is this – your user interface styles should be unified and consistent in one way or another, be it color, textures, shapes, or something else entirely.

Style fonts

The font style defines has a big impact on the look and feel of the element it is applied to. Text in a user interface is one of the first things the user sees. Humans are drawn to text because it informs them of what they're looking at. If readability is important (and it is), some fonts are better suited than others for a web application.

The font type is the most effective way to change how the text is read. Our todo list widget, we set the font type using the `font-family` style property. We use this property to specify a list of font types we want to use in the style. It would be nice if all fonts were supported on every operating system. browsers. Sadly, this isn't the case. New fonts can be installed on your computer using operating system utilities, and some fonts will be installed automatically by applications such as Word or Photoshop. Our font type preference should be placed toward the beginning of the list.

Our todo list widget styles also changed the size of the font. This is also an important property to set when readability is a concern. Fonts that are too large don't use space effectively. Fonts that are too small leave too much empty space. In both cases, they're difficult to read.

Both the font type and font size you choose to use in your styles should be consistent. Web applications shouldn't use different font families. Using different font sizes should emphasize the level of importance different sections of text have. Headings should always be larger than the rest of the text. Paragraph-level text should always be the same size. Consistent font types along with consistent font sizes are the basis for formatting text with themes.

Theme basics

Our todo list widget has some basic styles applied to it. We've changed the font, the background and foreground colors, as well as the border. The widget also has some spacing applied to it. These style properties changed the look and feel of the widget from something plain to something that looks appealing.

The styles were applied to the HTML elements of the todo list by ID. There is a one-to-one correspondence using this method. The `#container` style can only apply to page elements with a container ID. This is a limitation we can do without. Reserving a style for a single element isn't ideal when designing theme styles. This approach leads to redundancy.

 We can use CSS selectors to apply a set of style properties to more than one element. Using CSS selectors effectively is an important aspect of creating themeable user interfaces, as we'll see in this section.

Time for action - grouping styles

Let's make some changes to our todo list example. We can start by removing some duplicate code in our style definitions. We do this by applying a style to a group of elements instead of just a single element:

1. Open the `style.css` file we created in the previous todo list example and replace the contents with the following:

```
#container {

    background: #f2f5f7;
```

```
    border: 3px solid #dddddd;
    width: 25%;
    padding: 3px;

}

#todo-title {

    color: #222222;
    padding-left: 5%;

}

#todo-list {

    font-size: 0.8em;
    color: #362b36;
    list-style-type: square;

}

h3, ul {

    font-family: Lucida Grande, Lucida Sans, Arial, sans-serif;

}
```

2. Open the `index.html` file from our todo list example in a web browser. You'll notice the page hasn't changed in appearance.

What just happened?

Let's walk through the code and see what we've done. In `style.css`, you'll notice we have a new style definition: `h3, ul`.

The `h3, ul` style sets the `font-family` property. The value of the property hasn't changed from the previous example. The font type will stay the same. This style is applied to the `h3` and `ul` elements in our todo list widget.

The `#container` style hasn't changed at all. The `#todo-title` and `#todo-list` styles no longer define a `font-family` property. This is now handled by our new `h3, ul` style and is only set once instead of twice.

Repetitive style properties

We saw how we can eliminate a repetitive style property. By creating a new style that is applied to more than one element, we only need to define a property once. Our todo list is a simple widget, without many parts. Imagine we had something more complex with 10 or more HTML elements. If they all shared a common style property, such as `font-family`, we wouldn't want to set the property ten times.

Not only is this an inconvenience for the theme author, it also leads to bugs in our styles. If we have to remember to change a property more than once to change the look and feel of a single widget, this widens the opportunity for error. Redundant style properties also lead to a larger stylesheet. Not only does it look bad, but these files need to be downloaded. Compactness is a virtue.

Group selectors

The new style we just added to our todo list widget, `h3, ul`, is actually two CSS selectors. The comma between the `h3` and `ul` in the style definition is a separator between selectors. It tells the web browser to apply the properties of this style to each selector. Grouped styles are applied in multiple steps, in our case two. First, the `h3` elements are styled, followed by the `ul` elements. This process repeats itself for however many selectors we have grouped together. We can have as many selectors grouped together as we please. In practice, however, we don't want more than a few because your styles will be hard to maintain.

Themes for Web user interfaces can use grouped CSS selectors to share common style properties. Our todo list widget used group selectors to set the `font-family` in one place, while maintaining consistency. However, group selectors have their drawbacks. We are able to remove a redundant style property from our todo list styles, but we introduced a new style. We now have four styles for our widget instead of three. This means we have another style to maintain instead of keeping the properties in an encapsulated unit. Another problem with our approach is that we're applying styles by element type instead of by ID. This means that all `h3` and `ul` elements on the page will be affected by our style, which may not be what we want. A better approach might be to reference elements by class rather than element ID or element type.

Have a go hero

Experiment with grouping by element ID. For example, our todo list widget style uses a group selector `h3, ul`. Try changing this to `#todo-title, #todo-list`. Do you get the same result?

Time for action - nesting styles

The last changes we made to our todo list example showed us how to remove duplicate CSS properties. We have a better control of how we apply styles to our widget, if we can classify the HTML elements within. Our todo list widget has an outer container that holds the widget content. Let's see if we can use this to our advantage:

1. Open the `index.html` file we created in our todo list example and replace the contents with the following:

```
<html xmlns="http://www.w3.org/1999/xhtml">
    <head>
        <title>Todo List</title>
        <link href="style.css" rel="stylesheet" type="text/css" />
    </head>
    <body>
        <div class="todo-list">
            <h3>TODO</h3>
            <ul>
                <li>Design user interface</li>
                <li>Implement form validation</li>
                <li>Deploy</li>
            </ul>
        </div>
    </body>
</html>
```

2. Open the `style.css` file we created in our todo list example and replace the contents with the following:

```
.todo-list {
    font-family: Lucida Grande, Lucida Sans, Arial, sans-serif;
    background: #f2f5f7;
    border: 3px solid #dddddd;
    width: 25%;
    padding: 3px;
```

```
    }

    .todo-list h3 {

        color: #222222;
        padding-left: 5%;

    }

    .todo-list ul {

        font-size: 0.8em;
        color: #362b36;
        list-style-type: square;

    }
```

3. Open the `index.html` file from our todo list example in a web browser. You'll notice that nothing has changed in appearance.

What just happened?

Let's walk through the code and see what we've changed.

In `index.html`, we've removed all `id` attributes. The container `div`, the title `h3`, and the list `ul` elements can no longer be referenced by ID. Instead, we've added a class attribute with the value of `todo-list` to the container `div`.

In `style.css`, we have three new styles for our todo list widget that have replaced the old ones. These are actually the same styles with new CSS selectors.

The `.todo-list` style replaces the `#container` style. It has the same style properties with the addition of the `font-family` property. We set the `font-family` property here because it will cascade downward, all contained elements will inherit the font style.

The `.todo-list h3` style replaces the `#todo-title` style. It sets the `color` and `padding-left` style properties of our todo list title.

The `.todo-list ul` style replaces the `#todo-list` style. It sets the `color`, the `font-size`, and `list-style-type` style properties of our todo list items.

Nested selectors

We've made some pretty drastic changes to our todo list widget with the latest modifications. We can no longer reference our elements by ID. We can, however, reference the widget HTML elements by class. This is what the dot in front of our style names denotes.

Nested selectors allow us to start with a general category and refine the selector criteria. The general category can apply style properties that are shared amongst elements nested within that general category. For instance, the `.todo-list` style is a general category that will select all elements with a `todo-list` class attribute. What if we want to define style properties for specific elements inside the `.todo-list` container? The general selector can is refined by adding a nesting level. The space in the selector indicates the latter element is nested in the former.

Classifying HTML elements that are widget components and using nested CSS selectors are an important aspect of theming web user interfaces. The `.todo-list` style ensures that the `font-family` property is consistent for all todo list widgets. We could take this a step further and create a class that is used not only by todo list widgets, but all widgets in our application. A generic style that applies to all widgets is the essence of theme style design.

Nesting depth

Our todo list widget only uses two levels of nesting in its styles. This is because there are only two levels of nesting in the HTML elements that we want to style. We have a container `div` and directly beneath, we have a `h3` and `ul` element. If we wanted to style the individual todo list items, we could define a style that looks like `.todo-list ul li`. This style has three levels of nesting and is still readable. Beyond that, things become more difficult to maintain and comprehend. Moreover, it becomes a performance problem, as the deeper the nesting, the slower the browser becomes, as it needs to drill down and apply the styles accordingly.

If you find that you're starting to add more than two or three levels of nesting to your style definitions, it's probably time to rethink your HTML structure. Alternatively, you may want to think about generalizing more style properties into a top-level CSS class that is applied to all your widgets. This is precisely how theme styles work.

Have a go hero

Try creating a nested class style. For example, try giving the `ul` element in our todo list its own class. Modify the `.todo-list ul` style to reference the new class instead of the `ul` element.

Pop quiz - theme basics

1. How do you remove a duplicate CSS style property?

    a. A duplicate CSS property can be reduced to a single property by creating a group selector that applies the property to multiple elements.

    b. Simplify the HTML structure so that it doesn't require duplicate CSS properties.

    c. Use classes instead of Ids to reference the HTML elements in your style definitions.

2. What are some of the drawbacks to using group selectors?

    a. A group selector introduces new style definitions, as opposed to a smaller number of styles to maintain.

    b. Group selectors introduce a noticeable performance loss in the web browser.

    c. Group selectors require the same type of HTML element for each member of the group.

3. What is the role of a generic style when using nested selectors?

    a. A generic, top-level style ensures consistency with style properties while the nested styles within set more specific style properties that aren't shared between the widget's elements.

    b. Generic selectors are too limiting because the properties they define can't be overridden.

    c. Cascading styles are only valid when they reference elements by ID.

Theme layout

Widgets in a web user interface aren't placed randomly on the page. Instead, they're in a predictable order, relative to other widgets. Alignment, spacing, position—these are all layout aspects that need to be considered when designing a theme.

More important than the page layout as a whole, theme layout is more concerned with the placement of HTML elements inside widgets. Our todo list widget contains HTML elements and we've given them padding. This is part of the widget layout. Here we will take a closer look at the role layout plays in themes.

Time for action - placing elements on the page

Let's modify our todo list widget to include a due date. It's great to have a todo list; it's even better if it eventually gets done. We'll update our widget theme styles to position the due date element within the widget.

1. Open the `index.html` file from the previous todo list examples and replace the content with the following:

```
<html xmlns="http://www.w3.org/1999/xhtml">
    <head>
        <title>Todo List</title>
        <link href="style.css" rel="stylesheet" type="text/css" />
    </head>
    <body>
        <div class="todo-list">
            <div class="due-date">Due - Last Week</div>
            <h3>TODO</h3>
            <ul>
                <li>Design user interface</li>
                <li>Implement form validation</li>
                <li>Deploy</li>
            </ul>
        </div>
    </body>
</html>
```

2. Open the `style.css` file from the previous *todo list* examples and replace the content with the following:

```
.todo-list {

    font-family: Lucida Grande, Lucida Sans, Arial, sans-serif;
    background: #f2f5f7;
    border: 3px solid #dddddd;
    width: 25%;
    padding: 3px;

}

.todo-list h3 {

    color: #222222;
    padding-left: 5%;
```

```
    }

    .todo-list ul {

        font-size: 0.8em;
        color: #362b36;
        list-style-type: square;

    }

    .due-date {

        float: right;
        font-size: 0.7em;
        color: #362b36;

    }
```

3. Open the `index.html` file in a web browser:

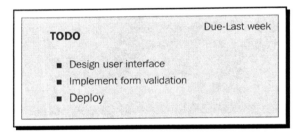

What just happened?

Let's walk through the code and see what we've changed.

In `index.html`, we've added a new `div` element that holds the due date text. This `div` has a class attribute `due-date`.

In `style.css`, we've created a new style, `.due-date`. This style sets the `float` property to `right`. This will position the due date `div` to the right-hand side of the todo list container `div`. The `font-size` property is set to be slightly smaller than the rest of the font in the widget and the color is set to be the same as the list items.

Layout design

We've positioned the new feature of our todo list widget, the due date, in the top right-hand side corner. The positioning of this new element is the responsibility of the theme. Before the due date was added, our todo list elements were positioned by the HTML that defines them. Here we're using the `float` property to move the element to the right of the containing element. If we hadn't specified this property in our theme styles, the due date would be displayed to the left-hand side and above the todo list title.

 The `float` CSS property is a good way to position HTML elements, especially for those that are the constituents of widgets. If there isn't room to position the element to the right-hand side, it will be pushed downward.

We're not restricted in how we choose to position elements in our themes. There are several ways we could have placed the due date where we did. The nice thing about the `float` property is that there aren't any pixel or percentage values, which increase the chance for inconsistency.

Consistent layout

Users don't want to use an application with inconsistent user interface layouts. When a layout is inconsistent, we lose the predictability of where widgets can be found. Once you've been using an application for a day or two, you become familiar with where things are located. This familiarization takes longer if one widget is aligned differently from another widget. For instance, if we had another widget with a due date that was aligned to the left-hand side, this would be hard to digest.

This is where layout in themes come into play. If we were to create another widget that had a due date, we would want to use the `.due-date` style we created for our todo list widget. The due date in other widgets would get the some fonts, the same colors, but it would also get the layout. This is something that is difficult to get right when trying to align elements in a consistent way using HTML alone.

Have a go hero

Try changing the positioning in the `.due-date` style. For example, the requirements of your theme have changed—the due date for todo list widgets should always be displayed in the bottom right-hand side corner. (Hint: you may need to use position: relative in the `.due-date` style).

Pop quiz - theme layout

1. How is using the float property beneficial in comparison to other positioning properties?

    a. The `float` property positions elements relative to their container element. This negates the need for pixel or percentage values and reduces the chance of human error.

    b. The `float` property can only be expressed as a percentage; this is a more accurate way of positioning elements.

    c. The `float` property has better browser support than other positioning properties such as left and top.

2. Why is it better to position widget elements in a CSS theme instead of in the HTML?

    a. Different widgets in a user interface can share a style, including layout properties. This makes it easier for theme authors to create a consistent layout.

    b. Themes shouldn't define any layout information, only colors.

    c. Theme layout is the the most important part of a theme, everything else is secondary.

jQuery UI themes

Now that we have a better understanding of what widgets and themes are, and how they relate to one another, we can take a look at the jQuery UI JavaScript framework.

jQuery UI is actually two sub-frameworks. A widget framework consisting of a widget factory and a set of commonly used widgets. A CSS framework that defines the look and feel of all widgets created with the latter. The CSS framework provides the basis to create themes, in addition to the themes that ship with jQuery UI, and is the basis of this book.

The widget framework

The jQuery UI widget framework has a selection of widgets we can choose from. These widgets are general enough to be used in most application categories such as finance or e-commerce. For instance, the tabs widget is useful for navigating the logical sections of your application. The button widget is universally recognized as an action taking place when clicked.

We can also use the widget framework to define our own widgets. For instance, our todo list widget we've been working with in this chapter could be created as a jQuery UI widget by using the **widget factory**. We can also use the widget factory to extend the capabilities of the existing widgets. For example, we could extend the progress bar widget to behave differently when the user hovers over it.

The CSS framework

The jQuery UI CSS framework is a collection of styles. What makes this set of styles a framework is the naming convention used. Each style in the framework is defined as a CSS class. So while these styles can be applied to any element in a web page, they were designed with the intent of being applied to widgets created using the framework.

The naming conventions used by the CSS classes in the framework are how jQuery UI themes are able to function in any jQuery UI application. A widget created with the jQuery UI widget framework has one or more CSS framework classes assigned to its HTML elements. This is how widgets get their look and feel.

Theme-ready widgets

Any jQuery UI widget is theme-ready. That is, it honors styles defined within the constraints of the CSS framework. This is only possible because of the separation of the widget and CSS framework. If the styles of each widget were defined in the widgets themselves, it would be difficult, if not impossible, to change the look and feel of the application.

When it comes time to change themes in a jQuery UI application, the widgets aren't even aware that this has happened. The theme is separated into an entirely different layer from that of the widgets. If our todo list widget were to change themes, there would be a lot of work to do. The first problem is that there is no indication that it is actually a widget that is theme-ready. We have to manually ensure that the HTML elements of the widget have the correct classes.

Summary

In this chapter, we learned a lot about widgets, themes, and styles in general. These are essential ingredients for creating themeable user interfaces. Widgets are the structural components that user interfaces are made of. Styles change the look and feel of widgets in addition to the layout of the widget elements.

Adding styles to widgets presents problems with consistency and portability. We've seen different ways we can improve our CSS so that we can avoid duplicate property definitions by grouping selectors. We can further increase style reuse by moving CSS properties to a base class and nesting more specific properties within it.

Layout also plays a role in designing themes. The individual HTML elements that make up a widget need to be positioned properly and given appropriate space. These are all things that should be controlled by the theme styles. The HTML structure says what the widget has, while the theme says where it goes.

The jQuery UI framework helps us with all concepts learned in this chapter. The two sub-frameworks provided by jQuery UI give us widgets as well as a CSS framework we can use to create our own themes.

In the next chapter, we'll dig a little deeper into how jQuery UI theming works and get hands-on examples and experience with the framework.

2
Using Themes

Putting themes to use with jQuery UI is the goal of this chapter. Once you've used a jQuery UI theme in an HTML page, changing that theme is easy. We've seen what themes are and why they are useful.

In this chapter we shall:

◆ Download jQuery UI with a theme

◆ Discuss the overall theme structure

◆ Walk through theming a page

◆ Use the theme switcher

◆ Compare jQuery UI theming to other frameworks

Let's put themes to use.

Downloading jQuery UI

Before we can start using jQuery UI, we need to download it. There are several options on the jQuery UI download page that allow you to customize which components you use.

Time for action - building a download

Let's walk through downloading jQuery UI.

1. Direct your web browser to `http://jqueryui.com/download`.

2. On the right-hand side of the page, you'll see a content box that allows you to select a theme and the jQuery UI version. Select a theme or use the default selection. Don't change any other options.

3. Click on the **Download** button. Your browser will then prompt you to save `jquery-ui-1.8.x.custom.zip`. Save the file on your local hard drive and extract the contents:

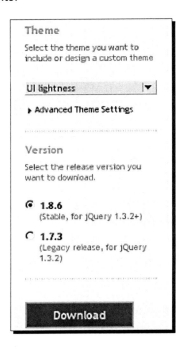

What just happened?

We've just downloaded jQuery UI using the default download settings. We've extracted the ZIP archive that contains all the jQuery UI files. These include the widget JavaScript files and the theme CSS files.

Throughout this book, we'll be referring to jQuery UI version numbers as 1.8.x and jQuery core version numbers as 1.5.x. The examples in this book will work with all bug-fix releases of jQuery UI 1.8. When working with the code examples, be sure to replace the x with the appropriate number. By default, the current stable version of jQuery UI is selected for download. We could have selected to download jQuery UI 1.7.x, which is the legacy version. This is only useful if you need to support a user interface created with an older version.

The contents of the `css` folder in the jQuery UI package depend on your theme selection. For instance, if I selected `ui-lightness` as my theme, the `css` folder will contain a `ui-lightness` folder with all the CSS files used to implement the theme.

Something we didn't look at was the Advanced Theme Settings in the jQuery UI download configuration. These options allow you to set the CSS scope and the theme folder name. These can be helpful if you're planning on using multiple themes in your application but are usually not necessary.

Minimal downloads

On the jQuery UI download page there are several check boxes that we ignored during the previous example. These are the individual components that comprise jQuery UI. By default, all components are selected, which is generally what we want to do. However, if you're using jQuery UI for only one or two widgets, there is no need for everything else.

Time for action - removing downloaded components

Let's modify our jQuery UI download to use a couple of widgets.

   1. Click on the **Deselect** all components link near the top of the page. The selected components to the right-hand side should say 0 of 31 selected and the Download button will be disabled.

   2. In the **Widget** section, select the **Accordion and Tabs** checkboxes.

   3. Click on the **Download** button. Your browser will then prompt you to save `jquery-ui-1.8.x.custom.zip`. Save the file on your local hard drive and extract the contents:

☑ **Accordion**	Creates an accordion navigation widget.	
☐ **Autocomplete**	Creates an autocomplete widget.	
☐ **Button**	Creates an button widget.	
☐ **Dialog**	Opens existing markup in a draggable and resizable dialog.	
☐ **Slider**	A flexible slider with ranges and accessibility via keyboard.	
☑ **Tabs**	Transforms a set of container elements into a tab structure.	
☐ **Datepicker**	A datepicker than can be toggled from a input or displayed inline.	
☐ **Progressbar**	A status indicator that can be used for a loading state and standard percentage indicators.	

What just happened?

This version of the jQuery UI download is much smaller than the previous example (260KB vs 1001KB to be exact). This is because we have selected only two widgets to download, **Accordion** and **Tabs**. By default, all jQuery UI widgets are selected for download. This is because you would need to know ahead of time which widgets you don't need. This is rarely the case.

Downloading a minimal copy of jQuery UI not only reduces the size of the Javascript files, but the size of the theme CSS files too. The benefit is that there is less CSS to maintain for your theme. The drawback is that we need to download jQuery UI again if we realize we're missing a widget. It is almost always better to download the full copy of jQuery UI. Only customize your download when and if the JavaScript and CSS file sizes become an issue.

Theme structure

It is now time for us to take a deeper look at what we've downloaded. It is worthwhile knowing what the files and directories inside the jQuery UI package represent. There are certain aspects that are more relevant than others. In our case, we care more about theming-related files and how they relate to widgets used by other developers.

Development bundle

You'll notice from our previous example that the extracted contents of the jQuery UI package are three directories: `css`, `js`, and `development-bundle`. The `css` and `js` directories are production copies of the development bundle files. In `css`, for instance, you'll find a theme directory (the name of the selected theme during download). Within the theme folder, we have an images directory and a single `jquery-ui-1.8.x.css` file. If we were using this package in a production environment, we'd simply include the single CSS file in order to have access to all our widget theme styles.

The `development-bundle` folder is different. This is where you'll find CSS theme files suitable for editing. Let's take a brief walk through it:

◆ In the `development-bundle` folder, you'll find a `themes` folder. This is where all your jQuery UI themes under development are stored.

◆ In the `themes` folder, similar to the production `css` folder, you'll find a folder with the name of your selected theme. For example, lightness or redmond.

◆ Also in the **themes** folder, there is another folder called `base`. This is another theme that always exists in the `development-bundle` folder, no matter what theme you selected during download. The base theme is a plain theme, similar to smoothness that you can use as a starting point to build your own.

◆ If you open your `themes` folder, you'll notice another difference between the `development-bundle` and production `css` folders—there are plenty more CSS files here. These are all the theme-related CSS files for jQuery UI widgets.

File structure

Let's take a moment and discuss the file structure within the `themes` folder of the `development-bundle`. This is where we'll make changes to themes that we either design from scratch or use existing themes as a starting point. The following diagram gives an idea of the theme-related files used in the jQuery UI `development-bundle`:

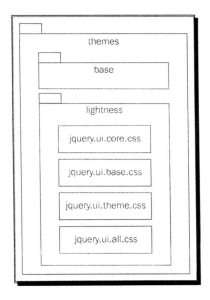

We can see in this diagram that all theme-related CSS files are in the `lightness` folder, as that is the theme we selected when jQuery UI was downloaded. You'll also notice that we haven't listed all files in the `themes` folder; only those that are central to changing themes. Let's take a look at the role each file plays:

◆ The `jquery.ui.all.css` file is what ties everything together with regard to theme styles. The file uses the `@import` CSS directive to include the `jquery.ui.base.css` and `jquery.ui.theme.css` files.

◆ The `jquery.ui.base.css` file is "glue" file—it contains nothing but CSS imports that tie everything together. It imports the `jquery.ui.core.css` file as well as the individual jQuery UI widget styles.

◆ The `jquery.ui.core.css` file provides some foundation styles that are shared amongst different widget types. They are helper classes that help with common visibility and positioning issues that any theme will need, regardless of how it looks.

◆ Finally, `jquery.ui.theme.css` gives widgets in a jQuery UI application their common look and feel. The CSS styles defined here are shared among all built-in jQuery UI widgets and should also be used by custom widgets. If you look at some of the style names, widget, state, icon, and so on, you'll notice that they're purposefully generic. These are the types of things all widgets have that define how they look.

Class structure

Before we start using jQuery UI, let's take a closer look at some of the CSS styles found in `jquery.ui.theme.css`. Conceptually, we can categorize the most important CSS styles as **containers**, **states**, and **cues**.

The following diagram illustrates the essential container classes that define the container theme CSS styles:

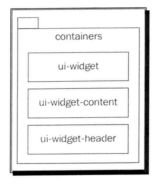

The CSS classes defined here are `ui-widget`, `ui-widget-container`, and `ui-widget-header`. These classes are used by every widget in a jQuery UI application.

The following diagram illustrates interaction state CSS classes used by the jQuery UI theme framework:

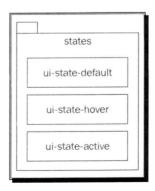

The state-related CSS classes are used by jQuery UI widgets to change the look of the widget when the user is interacting with it in some way.

The following diagram illustrates interaction cue CSS classes used by the jQuery UI theme framework:

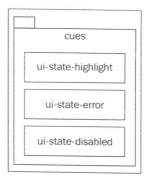

The cue-related CSS classes are used to change the visual state of a widget based on something that has happened in the application. This is different from an interaction state, which is usually changed directly by the user.

Using jQuery UI

So far in this chapter, we've seen how to download the jQuery UI package, how jQuery UI can be customized prior to downloading, and the basic theming constructs. Now we're ready to start building user interfaces so we can see themes in action.

Time for action - using widgets

We're now going to create our first themeable jQuery UI interface. It will be a simple one at that—a button widget, when clicked, displays a dialog widget:

1. Create a new `index.html` file with the following content:

```
<html xmlns="http://www.w3.org/1999/xhtml">

    <head>

        <title>Hello Dialog</title>

        <link href="jqueryui/css/ui-lightness/jquery-ui-
1.8.x.custom.css" rel="stylesheet" type="text/css" />

        <script type="text/javascript" src="jqueryui/js/jquery-
1.5.x.min.js"></script>
```

```
        <script type="text/javascript" src="jqueryui/js/jquery-ui-
1.8.x.custom.min.js"></script>11
        <script type="text/javascript" src="index.js"></script>

    </head>
    <body style="font-size: 10px;">
        <button id="btn_hello">Say Hello</button>
        <div id="dlg_hello">Hello World!</div>
    </body>
</html>
```

2. Make sure there is a jqueryui folder in the same folder as index.html. It should have the same contents as was extracted from the jQuery UI package downloaded earlier in the chapter.

3. Create a new index.js file with the following content:

```
$(document).ready(function(){

    $("#dlg_hello").dialog( { autoOpen: false });

    $("#btn_hello").button().click(function(){ $("#dlg_hello").
dialog("open"); });

});
```

4. Open index.html in a web browser. You should see a **Say Hello** button:

5. Clicking on the **Say Hello** button should open a dialog widget, seen as follows:

What just happened?

We've just created our first two widgets with jQuery UI! We've created two new files to implement our example - `index.html` defines our page structure and defines the JavaScript used to create the widgets.

In `index.html`, we set a global style setting in the body element—`font-size: 10px;`. This will set the font size to `10px` for any elements displayed on this page, including jQuery UI widgets. The reason we're setting this style property here is because this is an example and we don't want to set up a new style sheet for just one property.

Inside the `body` tag, we have two elements - a `button` and a `div`:

◆ The button element serves as a template for the button widget. The code in `index.js`—`$('btn_hello').button()`—creates the widget.

◆ The `div` element serves as a template for the dialog widget. The code in `index.js`—`$('dlg_hello').dialog()`—creates the widget.

You'll notice that everything in the `index.js` module is surrounded by a `$(document).ready()` callback function. This is important; we cannot create our widgets until the page has finished loading. Any jQuery UI widget relies on an HTML element—its template. If the template isn't ready, jQuery UI doesn't know how to create the widget. Creating widgets inside `$(document).ready()` is a safe way to ensure the required HTML elements are available.

The first widget we create is the dialog. When our example page loads, you'll notice that the dialog `div` isn't displayed anywhere. This is because we've passed an option to the dialog constructor, `autoOpen`, which tells it to remain hidden initially.

The second widget created is the button. We don't pass any arguments to the button constructor. The `.button()` call returns a copy of the button widget. On the same line, we use `.click()` to tell the button we want something to happen when the user clicks on the button. In our example, our supplied function to `.click()` displays the dialog widget by calling `..dialog("open")`.

Have a go hero - change the dialog options

The dialog widget has plenty of options available for the developer. Try adding options to the dialog constructor in the example above to give the dialog a title and make the dialog modal. A list of available dialog options can be found here: `http://jqueryui.com/demos/dialog/`.

Pop quiz - using jQuery UI

1. Why do widget constructors need to be called inside $(document).ready()?

    a. The $(document).ready() runs the callback after all HTML elements have finished loading. This is required in order for jQuery UI widgets to function correctly.

    b. The jQuery UI library isn't loaded until $(document).read() is called.

    c. Creating widgets inside $(document).ready() isn't a requirement, it's just good practice.

2. How would I call a 'doSomething' method on a "sample" widget?

    a. $("#myid").sample("doSomething")

    b. $("#myid").sample().doSomething()

    c. $("#myid").doSomething()

3. How do theme style properties get applied to widgets?

    a. Widgets are made up of DOM, or HTML elements. CSS classes from the jQuery UI CSS framework are applied to these underlying elements when the widget is created

    b. Widgets inherit theme style properties through the widget HTML.

    c. Widget theme style properties are manually applied with the jQuery css() function.

Widget options

In the preceding example, we passed an option to the dialog widget constructor. Any options passed to a widget constructor are contained in a Javascript object. This is simply a key-value pair. Going back to the example, the object { autoOpen: false } specifies autoOpen as the key and false as the value. We can use as many key-value pairs inside a JavaScript object as we want. However, we'd only want to pass options to widget constructors that will be understood.

 Nearly every aspect of a widget can be controlled by passing options to the constructor. Widgets accept options that control their visibility, whether or not they're enabled, and callback functions for widget events. We can also control the appearance of widget with options that are passed at creation time. For instance, we could have specified a width for our dialog. Thankfully, jQuery UI widgets are smart enough to use an appropriate default for most options. The dialog widget alone has over 20 available options!

We're not limited to changing the various options offered by widgets to setting them in the constructor. Although, most of time, this is more convenient and readable. However, sometimes you can't avoid change a widget option until after it has been created. We can use widget methods to set and get options in addition to other things.

Widget methods

We've seen a widget method in action already. In our previous example, we used the `.dialog("open")` method to display our dialog widget. The confusing part is that this looks just like the constructor—instead of passing an options object, we're passing it a string. This is difficult to get used to if you've never used jQuery before but the rule is that any jQuery UI widget method looks like `.widget("method")`. The reason for this is that every jQuery UI widget is actually a jQuery plugin. Each plugin understands how to call its own methods as long as we use the mentioned form.

We can retrieve the value of any widget option that was set in the constructor after the widget is created using getter methods. Likewise, we can also use setter methods to update the value of an option. For instance, if we wanted to retrieve the value of the option we set in our example, we would call `.dialog("option", "autoOpen")`. In our case, this would return false, as this is what we set in the constructor. The option method serves as both the setter and the getter for any particular option. For instance, if we hadn't set the `autoOpen` option in the constructor and wanted to do it now, we would call `.dialog("option", "autoOpen", false)`.

Widgets also have a few other methods that are useful to the JavaScript application. For instance, we could call `.dialog("isOpen")` to see if it is currently being displayed. Some methods are common to all widget types. The destroy method is an example - all widgets can be created so we need a way to destroy them. When widgets are destroyed, this manipulates the underlying page **Document Object Model (DOM)**.

Widgets and the DOM

How do widgets relate to elements on the page? We're constructing the widgets with JavaScript, so how does that relate to the page? Any jQuery UI widget is composed of HTML elements. JavaScript uses the document object model, or DOM, to create and manipulate these elements on the fly. There are plenty of resources available that explain just what the DOM is and how it works.

As we saw in our previous example, jQuery UI widgets use DOM elements as templates. For instance, the button HTML element works perfectly well as a button, something the user can click and usually has a label. The jQuery UI button widget can use this button element as its blueprint. It is merely improving an existing element rather then reinventing the wheel.

Why does it matter which HTML widgets we used to create jQuery UI widgets? In our example, we used a `button` HTML element to create the button widget and a `div` element to create the dialog widget. There is no dialog HTML element unfortunately, so we need to use a general purpose element like a `div`. The `button` element, however, does the same thing as the jQuery UI button widget; it just doesn't look as good. jQuery UI widgets also share some aspects of the underlying DOM element, including the widget styles.

Widgets and CSS

You're probably wondering how all this relates to applying a theme to a widget. The jQuery UI theme framework defines all styles in classes. These classes are then applied to the widgets, indirectly, through the DOM. Widgets are made up of DOM elements so they can use them to define their look and feel.

It is the responsibility of the widget to apply the CSS classes required to display it properly. For instance, the two widgets we created in the example above, the button and the dialog, applied CSS classes to the HTML elements that make of the widget in the constructor. Many of the jQuery UI widgets will alter the starting element by adding new HTML elements inside. These new elements are in turn affected by the CSS classes applied to the widget.

Widgets can also be destroyed. This is done by calling the `.widget("destroy")` method. This will not remove the starting element used to create the jQuery UI widget. It only destroys visual changes made by the widget. For instance, if we were to call `.button("destroy")` in our example, the button would return to the normal HTML form. It will also remove any jQuery UI theme framework classes. This makes sense because we don't want the widget framework to remove elements that may be relevant to the application.

Switching themes

We're not restricted to using a single theme in our jQuery UI application. One of the great features of themes is that they're easily transported between applications. This feature is what enabled our earlier example to use any theme we selected in the jQuery UI download.

 When we're building jQuery UI applications, we can assume that the chosen theme will not be the final one used. And this is fine with us - we can switch jQuery UI themes with ease. Instead of downloading a new copy of jQuery UI during development every time we need to test a new theme, there are utilities we can use to update our theme dynamically. There's no need to manually download anything.

Time for action – exploring the theme switcher widget

Let's update our example above to include a theme-switcher widget:

1. Open the `index.html` file from the previous example in this chapter and replace the content with the following:

```
<html xmlns="http://www.w3.org/1999/xhtml">

    <head>

        <title>Hello Dialog</title>

        <link href="jqueryui/css/redmond/jquery-ui-1.8.x.custom.
css" rel="stylesheet" type="text/css" />

        <script type="text/javascript" src="jqueryui/js/jquery-
1.5.x.min.js"></script>

        <script type="text/javascript" src="jqueryui/js/jquery-ui-
1.8.x.custom.min.js"></script>

        <script type="text/javascript" src="http://jqueryui.com/
themeroller/themeswitchertool/"></script>

        <script type="text/javascript" src="index.js"></script>

    </head>

    <body style="font-size: 10px;">

        <div id="switcher" style="padding-bottom:10px;"></div>

        <button id="btn_hello">Say Hello</button>

        <div id="dlg_hello">Hello World!</div>

    </body>

</html>
```

2. Open the `index.js` file from the previous example in this chapter and replace the content with the following:

```
$(document).ready(function(){

    $('#switcher').themeswitcher();

    $("#dlg_hello").dialog( { autoOpen: false });

    $("#btn_hello").button().click(function(){ $("#dlg_hello").
dialog("open"); });

});
```

3. Open `index.html` in a web browser. You should see the new theme-switcher widget above our button:

4. Select a new theme and click on the **Say Hello** button.

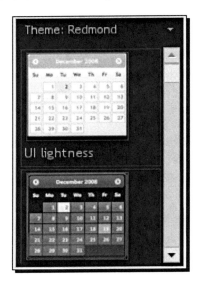

What just happened?

Our example now includes the theme-switcher widget as part of the user interface. To accomplish this, we've only made minor changes to our HTML and JavaScript files.

In `index.html`, we've included a new script, `http://jqueryui.com/themeroller/themeswitchertool/`. This script defines the theme-switcher widget. We've also added a new placeholder `div` element to place the new widget in. This is now the first element on the page. We give the `div` a CSS style property of `padding-bottom:10px` just to give our **Say Hello** button a little breathing room.

In `index.js`, we've added a new call to a widget constructor—`$('#switcher')`. `themeswitcher();`. This creates the theme-switcher widget in the same way as any other widget.

With these relatively minor adjustments, we can now see how our user interface looks with different themes applied to it. Using the theme-switcher widget during development has some great benefits. First of all, we don't have to download a theme to see how it looks with our user interface. The jQuery UI theme files are retrieved behind the scenes when a theme is selected. Second, this is a great way to get feedback from non-technical users who would otherwise be reluctant to try different themes. The widget is so simple that anyone can very quickly figure out how it works.

However, the theme-switcher widget is better suited as a development tool instead of a widget that is part of a finished product in production. The main reason for this is that the theme-switcher widget relies on theme files that exist on a remote server. If something were to go wrong, this is out of your control. Additionally, you may not want to have users change themes dynamically. Once you find a theme that looks good, you're better off sticking with it.

Time for action - themeroller dev tool

The jQuery UI framework provides us with another way to switch themes without having to manually download the Themeroller dev tool. Let's set this tool up so we can see it in action:

1. The Themeroller dev tool only works with the Firefox browser. If you don't already have it installed, you can find installation instructions and download links at `http://www.mozilla.com/en-US/firefox/`.

2. Using Firefox, open `http://jqueryui.com/themeroller/developertool/`. You'll see instructions that show you how to drag the developer tool into your Firefox toolbar.

> ⊡ ThemeRoller Dev Tool

3. You should now have a ThemeRoller dev tool link in your Firefox toolbar. Point your browser to `http://jqueryui.com/demos/accordion/` and click on the dev tool link. You will see a new dialog open that allows you to change themes or design your own:

What just happened?

The previous example was probably much simpler if you already had Firefox installed. The Themeroller dev tool only works with Firefox due to security restrictions. If you try to use it with another browser, you'll see a message stating this.

We've demonstrated how we can add the link that displays the dev tool into the Firefox toolbar. We then opened the accordion widget demo page on the jQuery UI site. The Themeroller dev tool allows us to switch themes for jQuery UI widgets on any page. This is different from the theme switcher widget in that we didn't need to change our application to enable theme changes. This means that anyone with Firefox installed can view your jQuery UI application using a different theme!

The Themeroller dev tool has a feature that the theme-switcher widget doesn't—a **built-in theme roller**. The theme roller lets us build our own themes and is the subject of focus in the next chapter.

Pop quiz - switching themes

1. How do the jQuery UI theme-switching utilities help with the development process?

    a. The jQuery UI theme-switching utilities speed along the user interface development process by negating the need to download a theme manually for testing purposes. We can also get fast feedback from non-technical users.

    b. The theme-switching utilities don't help; they only slow down the development process.

    c. Switching themes during the development process eliminates the need to download themes at all from the jQuery UI website.

2. What is the difference between the theme-switcher widget and the ThemeRoller dev tool?

    a. The theme-switcher widget needs to be inserted into the user interface code while the ThemerRoller dev tool is a bookmark that goes in the Firefox toolbar.

    b. The ThemeRoller dev tool needs to be inserted into the user interface code while the theme-switcher widget is a bookmark that goes in the Firefox toolbar.

    c. The theme-switcher widget is more stable than the ThemeRoller dev tool.

Other frameworks

jQuery UI isn't the only JavaScript toolkit that supports themeable widgets. There are several other libraries based on jQuery that display widgets. The trouble with these is that they lack any kind of theme support. This is why jQuery UI is the official user interface library for jQuery applications.

However, jQuery isn't the only JavaScript library in existence. Let's take a brief look at a couple others to see how they do theming.

Dojo

The dojo toolkit is similar to the jQuery JavaScript toolkit - they're both divided into sub-frameworks. Dojo has a core framework as well as a widget framework called Dijit. The Dijit framework also has an underlying CSS framework similar to that of jQuery UI.

The main difference between the jQuery UI and Dijit frameworks isn't how theming works but in size and complexity. Dijit, and Dojo as a whole, are much larger than jQuery UI and jQuery respectfully. If you're looking to implement a user interface that is lightweight, jQuery UI is usually a better choice. The Dijit widget system comes with four pre-built themes. jQuery UI has 24.

For more information see `http://dojotoolkit.org/`.

Ext JS

The Ext JS JavaScript toolkit is similar to Dojo. It is a full-featured framework with every widget you would possibly want to use included. It is very well documented and has both open source versions as well as proprietary releases. If you require professional support this might be an option for you. Widgets are also themeable but this isn't well documented.

Ext JS has the same problems as Dojo—they are both large and complex. Building a full-featured application with these toolkits involves a time investment in learning.

For more information see `http://www.sencha.com/products/js/`

Other JavaScript widget toolkits don't have the same focus on theming as the jQuery UI framework. A lot of work has gone into designing the CSS class structure in such a way as to be extensible for every widget created, including custom widgets. It is also handy that we have tools at our disposal to quickly design themes and that is the topic of the next chapter.

Summary

In this chapter, we've walked through the process of downloading jQuery UI with a theme. You can customize more than just the theme - individual jQuery UI components may be selected for download. The jQuery UI CSS framework isn't just a handful of CSS classes. Rather, there is a structured hierarchy that allows the styles to be applied universally.

We've seen how to include the jQuery UI components in a web page, the jQuery core, the jQuery UI widgets, and the CSS framework. We've created a couple of sample widgets and put them to use. Widgets are based on an underlying HTML element. We use these elements as a starting point for our widgets. The widget constructor can accept any number of parameters that alter the way the widget looks and behaves. jQuery UI widget methods are different from regular object methods. Each widget is actually a jQuery UI plugin and we pass the name of the method we want to call to the plugin constructor.

The development process of building a jQuery UI application is made easier by the utilities that help us change themes without the need to download them manually. We used the theme-switcher widget and the Themeroller Dev tool to do this.

Up until now, we've only used existing themes from the pre-built selection offered by jQuery UI.

In the next chapter, we'll take a closer look at the themeroller application and see how we can build our own theme.

3
Using the ThemeRoller

This chapter is all about the ThemeRoller application and how to roll your own jQuery UI themes. This is an indispensable tool for customizing user interfaces.

In this chapter, we shall:

- Get familiar with ThemeRoller
- Browse the theme gallery
- Explore theme settings
- Edit existing themes
- Download a theme

So let's get rolling.

ThemeRoller basics

Before we start using the ThemeRoller application to design and build our own themes, we'll take a quick look at what makes it such a handy tool. We saw our first glimpse of the ThemeRoller in the previous chapter, when we used the ThemeRoller dev tool inside Firefox. There is a lot more to the ThemeRoller than simply changing themes—we also use it to build them. You can think of it as an IDE for jQuery UI themes.

Instant feedback

What makes the ThemeRoller application such a powerful development tool is the speed with which you get feedback to changes made in the theme design. Any change made in the ThemeRoller is instantaneously reflected in the sample widgets provided on the page. For instance, if I were to change a font setting, that change would be reflected immediately in the sample widgets provided on the same page. There is no need to update the application you're building to see the results of small adjustments made to theme style settings.

The same is true of prepackaged themes in the ThemeRoller gallery. Selecting a theme will apply it to the same widgets - you get immediate feedback. This is very helpful in deciding on prepackaged themes. If you can see how it looks with jQuery UI widgets right away, that may dissuade you from using the theme or it may close the deal.

The idea behind this feedback mechanism offered by the ThemeRoller is a sped-up development cycle. Eliminating several steps when developing anything, themes included, is a welcome feature.

The dev tool

In the previous chapter, we introduced the ThemeRoller dev tool. It is a simple bookmarket for Firefox that brings the entire ThemeRoller application into any page with jQuery UI widgets. The benefit of the dev tool is that it allows you to see immediate theme changes in the context of the application you're building. If you use the ThemeRoller application from the jQuery UI website, you can only see changes as they apply to the sample widgets provided. This can give you a better idea of what the theme changes will look like on a finished product.

There are some limitations to using the dev tool though. If you're developing your application locally, not on a development server, you can't use the dev tool due to security restrictions. The dev tool is better suited for viewing changes to themes, or viewing different themes entirely, on a deployed user interface. Having said that, if you're designing a user interface with several collaborators, you might have a remote development server. In this scenario, the dev tool suits its name.

Portability

The ThemeRoller application is portable in more ways than one. The dev tool for Firefox allows us to use the application within any jQuery UI application. This means that we can design and tweak our jQuery UI themes as we build the widgets. This portability between applications means that we can build a single theme that works for a suite of applications, or a product line, if we're so inclined.

We can also use the ThemeRoller application directly from the jQueryUI website. This is handy if we don't have any widgets built or if you're trying jQuery UI out for the first time and just want to browse the wide selection of prepackaged themes.

Whatever approach you take, the application is the same and will always be consistent, as it is a hosted application. You don't need to concern yourself with installing an IDE for theme authors to collaborate with. The ThemeRoller application is available wherever they are.

ThemeRoller gallery

It is nice to have a wide variety of prepackaged themes to choose from. It isn't all that helpful if you can't see how they look. The ThemeRoller application has a gallery where we can not only browse prepackaged themes but also take them for a test drive. This section is about using the ThemeRoller gallery to view themes and get a feel of the variety available to us.

Viewing themes

The ThemeRoller application doesn't hide anything about the prepackaged themes in the gallery. When we preview a theme, we get to see how it looks when applied to widgets. The theme gallery even gives us a thumbnail in the browser to show a bird's eye view of the theme. So if you see a lot of black and you're looking for something bright, you don't need to bother selecting it to see how the widgets look with it.

Time for action - previewing a theme

It's time for us to preview a jQuery UI theme before we actually download it. We can get an idea of what a theme in the ThemeRoller gallery will look like when applied to widgets:

- ◆ Point your web browser to http://jqueryui.com/themeroller/.
- ◆ Select the **Gallery** tab in the **ThemeRoller** section on the right-hand side.
- ◆ Move your mouse pointer over any theme in the gallery. A visual indicator will be displayed.
- ◆ Select the theme thumbnail:

What just happened?

We've just selected a theme to preview from the ThemeRoller gallery. You'll notice that all the sample widgets to the right are instantly updated with the new theme. If we wanted to, we could change our theme selection and the sample widgets are once again updated with the theme changes.

You'll notice that once you make a theme selection, the URL in your address bar is now long and ugly. These are the individual theme settings for the chosen theme being passed to the ThemeRoller page with the sample widgets. You'll also notice that the theme selection on the left-hand side of the page isn't preserved. This is because we're passing individual theme settings and not the name of the theme itself, for example, instancetheme=darkness. We'll see why this distinction is important in a little bit.

Downloading themes

Once you've selected a theme from the gallery and you're happy with how it looks, it is time to download it and use it with your jQuery UI project. Downloading a theme is easy—each prepackaged theme has a download button that will take you to the jQuery UI download page. If we wanted to, we could download all themes in a single package to experiment with, locally. This would also eliminate the need for the ThemeRoller application, which you probably don't want to do.

Time for action - downloading a theme

The gallery is a nice way to preview a theme, but now we want to use it in our application. To do this, we need to download it. This is similar to downloading the jQuery UI toolkit:

1. Point your web browser to `http://jqueryui.com/themeroller/`.

2. Select the **Gallery** tab in the **ThemeRoller** section on the left-hand side.

3. Find a theme you wish to download. Click on the **Download** button underneath the theme thumbnail.

4. This will bring you to the jQuery UI download page. Notice that your chosen theme is selected on the right-hand side of the page.

5. Click on the **Download** button to download your theme:

What just happened?

We've just selected a prepackaged theme from the ThemeRoller gallery and downloaded it. This download page should look familiar from the previous chapter where we downloaded jQuery UI. In fact, you just downloaded jQuery UI again. The difference being, the downloaded ZIP archive contains the theme you selected from the gallery. The same principles apply for extracting the archive and using your theme with your jQuery UI application.

The downside is that if you're downloading a theme, chances are you already have a jQuery UI application under development. In this case, downloading jQuery UI JavaScript files is redundant. However, there is no easy way around this. This is one of the drawbacks to having a useful tool available to us—a minor drawback at that.

If you're only interested in the theme, you simply need to extract the theme folder from the ZIP archive and copy it to your jQuery UI application directory. You then need to update your path in your HTML in including the appropriate CSS file.

You'll also notice that after clicking on the **Download** button from the theme gallery, you're brought to the download page with an ugly URL. That is, you'll see something like `/downloa d/?themeParams=%3FffDefault` instead of just `/download`. This is a requirement of the ThemeRoller application that allows developers to edit existing themes or to roll their own. Without these parameters, we wouldn't be able to download themes we have made changes to.

The jQuery UI download page also includes an **Advanced Settings** section that is hidden by default. This is because you rarely need to use it. It allows you to set the CSS scope for your theme, useful if you're using multiple themes in a single user interface. This isn't a recommended practice; the key idea behind jQuery UI themes is consistency. The advanced settings also lets you change the name of the downloaded theme folder. This can be useful if you plan on changing your theme later, but you can always rename the folder after downloading it.

Pop quiz – ThemeRoller basics

1. Can you see what a jQuery UI theme looks like before downloading it?

   a. The ThemeRoller application provides a gallery of themes and a preview pane to the right containing sample widgets. When the theme selection changes, the theme is applied to the sample widgets.

   b. You can only see what a theme looks like after you've downloaded it and applied it to your widgets.

   c. You can only preview themes that have the preview option enabled on them.

2. How does ThemeRoller update the sample widgets with the currently selected theme settings?

   a. Whenever a theme setting is changed, the URL is updated. The URL is what defines the theme CSS applied to the preview widgets.

   b. There is a reload button at the top of the widget preview pane.

   c. When a theme setting is changed, an Ajax request is sent to the server which generates the new CSS style sheet. The response is then applied to the preview widgets.

3. How do you download jQuery UI with a theme from the ThemeRoller gallery?

   a. Each theme in the ThemeRoller gallery has a download button. This brings you to the jQuery UI download page with additional parameters that specify your desired theme settings.

   b. Each theme in the ThemeRoller gallery has a download button. This brings you to the jQuery UI download page with an additional theme parameter.

   c. If you want to use a theme from the ThemeRoller gallery, you must download it independently of jQuery UI.

Themes from scratch

So far, we've only been working with prepackaged themes. It is time to see how we can build our own themes from scratch. Every aspect of a theme can be adjusted from within the ThemeRoller; you don't have to write a single line of CSS to create your own theme. Because of the immediate feedback provided by the ThemeRoller, we don't need intimate knowledge of the inner workings of CSS to design the look and feel of a jQuery UI application.

When we start designing a theme from scratch, there is no starting point. That is, the ThemeRoller will fill in some initial values we'll most certainly want to change. The initial values are simply there so that the sample widgets have a theme applied to them when the page is loaded. Now we'll walk through these settings and watch the sample widgets change as we go.

Fonts

The fonts section of the ThemeRoller sets the font style properties for our theme. These settings apply to all widgets in which our theme is applied. It is thus important to select font settings that work well with other theme settings. Although this is the first group of theme settings we're changing, there is a good chance we'll be coming back to change them again to better reflect the changes we've made elsewhere in the theme. For instance, we may make some border thickness changes that make our chosen font settings tawdry by comparison. Another way to look at starting a new theme from scratch is to choose a font you're pleased with and use the font settings as the standard for all other theme settings.

Time for action - setting theme fonts

All fonts we see in a jQuery UI application are set in the theme style properties. Some themes share the same font settings while others are noticeably different from one another. We can define all these properties in the ThemeRoller application:

1. Point your web browser to `http://jqueryui.com/themeroller/`.

2. In the **ThemeRoller** section on the left-hand side of the page, expand the **Font Settings** section.

3. In the **Family** field, enter **Lucida Grande, Lucida Sans, Arial, Sans-serif**.

4. In the **Weight** field, select **bold**.

5. Leave the **Size** field as **1.1em**:

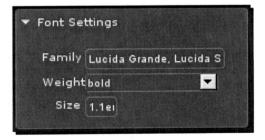

What just happened?

We've just taken our first steps toward creating our first custom theme using the ThemeRoller. We've set the **Family** property to use Lucida Grande as our first choice for the type of font to use in the theme. We've also changed the font weight to bold. We're happy with the default font size so we decided not to change it.

After making these changes, we're able to see the sample widgets on the right-hand side of the page are updated to reflect the new theme styles. Here is what the sample accordion widget looked like before the changes were made:

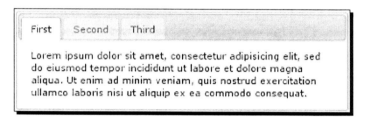

Here is the same sample widget after we made our theme font setting changes:

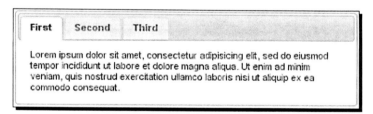

We can see the style of both the tab headers as well as the tab content has changed. The most noticeable change, however, was the font weight setting. The tab headers are now bold but the tab content isn't. The CSS framework makes a distinction in where it applies the font weight style. If the setting made all fonts bold, it would be very difficult to distinguish between header text and content text.

Corners

Almost every jQuery UI widget has corners and is thus affected by the theme corner settings. There is actually only one setting in the corners section - the corner radius. This determines the roundness of widget corners. Rounded corners look much better than straight lines. With this setting, we can give our theme slightly rounded corners or very rounded ones.

This setting relies on the CSS3 border-radius style property. This is supported by all major web browsers, except Internet Explorer 8 or earlier.

Time for action - changing the corner radius

You've probably noticed that all the sample widgets in the ThemeRoller application have rounded corners. This is a nice visual enhancement; most desktop environments have widgets with rounded corners. Straight corners can get boring after a while.

Something we can define in jQuery UI themes is the roundness of widget corners. That is, we can change the corner radius:

1. Continuing with our theme design, expand the **Corner Radius** section.

2. Change the value of the **Corners** field to 8px:

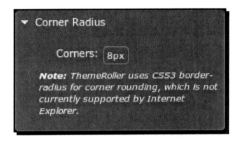

What just happened?

We've used the ThemeRoller to increase the roundness of our widget corners. The change may seem rather drastic - we've doubled the corner radius setting from 4px to 8px. The change, however, isn't overly sensational. Here is what the sample accordion widget looked like before the change was made:

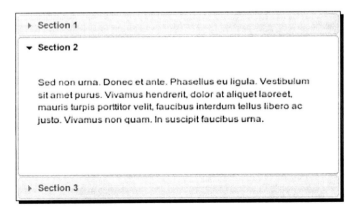

Here is what the sample accordion widget looks like after the change:

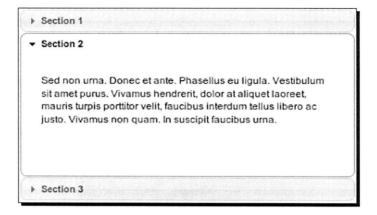

We can see that the corners of both the accordion header sections and the accordion content sections appear to be rounder.

In the **Corners** section of the ThemeRoller, there is a note explaining that corner roundness in jQuery UI themes is achieved by using the CSS3 border-radius style property. The only reason this is there is because this is a relatively new property that isn't supported by all browsers. IE still holds a large majority of the browser market share. Version 9 supports rounded corners but older IE versions do not. If you're targeting a specific browser with your jQuery UI application, check if this property is supported before investing too much time in designing beautifully rounded corners in your theme.

Headers

Just as a web page has a header, so do some jQuery UI widgets. The ThemeRoller allows us to set style properties for widget headers in our theme. Headers are meant to grab the attention of the user, just like headers in a web page. For instance, if I'm using a tabs widget, I'd want the names of each tab to stand out more than the content within the selected tab. In this section, we'll take a look at defining header theme settings.

Time for action - setting theme headers

It's time to give our theme some widget header styles. The ThemeRoller allows us to control the style properties for widget headers:

1. Continuing with our theme design, expand the **Header/Toolbar** section.

2. In the **Background color & texture** section, click on the small, colored square in the middle. This will open a texture selector.

3. Select the hard inset texture.

4. In the **Background color & texture** section, change the opacity from **75%** to **65%**.

5. In the **Border** setting, change the color value to **#828282**:

What just happened?

We've just set the widget header styles for our custom theme. The section is called Header/Toolbar because in some widgets, the distinction between header and toolbar is equivocal at best.

First, we updated the background color and texture settings. Actually, in our case, we've chosen to leave the background color as the default. There is nothing wrong with using default theme settings if that is what you want. We'll see that this is especially true when it comes to editing prepackaged themes later on. We did, however, change the background texture and opacity. We changed the texture to hard inset, which makes the header/toolbar background a fade toward the bottom. Any background texture is simply an image that overlays the header background color. We lowered the background opacity by 10%, or, increased the transparency by 10%. This simply changes the opacity of the background texture image.

Finally, we changed the header border color to something a little darker. Again, we decided to leave the text and the icon color settings alone. These will simply change the color of the header text and the header icon color respectfully.

Here is what the sample tabs widget looked like before we changed the header theme settings:

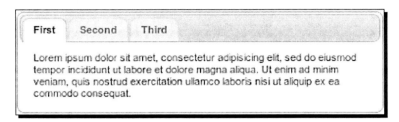

Here is what the sample tabs widget looks like after the header theme settings were changed:

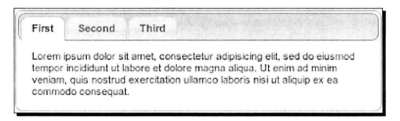

Here we can see that the border color of the header containing each individual tab is now slightly darker than the border of the tab widget. We can also see that the texture of the tabs header has been updated—it now fades toward the bottom.

Content

Content theme settings are the counterpart to header settings. Widgets that have a header usually have content as well. Remember, a header is used to convey what content follows. Header and content theme settings should be complimentary to a large degree. This is easy to do with the ThemeRoller as the settings in the two sections are identical.

Time for action - setting widget content styles

Now that we have header styles for our custom theme, it is time to define some widget content styles. We can use the ThemeRoller to set the content theme style properties. These are identical to the header settings:

1. Continuing with our theme design, expand the **Content** section.

2. In the **Background color & texture** section, select the background color selector to the left. Set the color to **#f5f5f4**.

3. In the **Background color & texture** section, select the background texture selector in the middle. Select the highlight soft texture.

4. In the **Border** setting, change the color value to **#828282**:

What just happened?

We've just set the content style settings for our theme. We changed the background color to something slightly darker than the default. We changed the widget content background texture to highlight soft. This changes the background so that it fades slightly at the top. The background looks good like this so we've left the content background opacity at 75%.

The content border color has been updated to something darker than the default. In fact, we've set the border color to be the same as the border color defined in the header section of the ThemeRoller. This way they complement one another. Also complementary to the header theme settings, are the content text and icon colors. We've left them as the default values.

Here is what the sample datepicker widget looked like before we changed the content theme settings:

Here is what the sample datepicker widget looks like after we update the content theme settings:

The outer border of the datepicker widget now matches that of the datepicker header. We can also notice the difference the background theme settings made.

States

jQueryUi widgets are always in one state or another. These states also play a role in themes. A widget in one state should look different than widgets in another state. These different appearances are controlled by CSS style properties within the theme.

States are especially prevalent in widgets that interact with mouse events. When a user hovers over a widget that is interested in these types of events, the widget changes into a hover state. When the mouse leaves the widget, it returns to a default state.

Even when nothing is happening with a widget—no events are taking place that the widget is interested in—the widget is in a default state. The reason we need a default state for widgets is so that they can return to their default appearance. The appearance of these states is entirely controlled through the applied theme. In this section, we'll change the ThemeRoller settings for widget states.

Time for action - setting default state styles

Some widgets that interact with the mouse have a default state applied to them. We can adjust how this state changes the appearance of the widget using ThemeRoller settings:

1. Continuing with our theme design, expand the **Clickable: default state** section.

2. In the **Background color & texture** section, click on the texture selector in the middle. Select the inset hard texture.

3. In the **Background color & texture** section, set the background opacity to 65%.

4. Change the **Border** color setting value to **#b0b0b0**.

5. Change the **Icon** color setting value to **#555555**:

What just happened?

We've just changed the look and feel of the default widget state. We changed the background texture to match that of the header theme settings. Likewise, we also changed the background opacity to 65%, also to match the header theme settings. The border color is now slightly darker - this looks better with the new default state background settings. Finally, the icon color was updated to match the default state font color.

Here is what the sample button looked like before we made our changes:

Here is what the sample button looks like after we've updated our theme settings:

Time for action - setting hover state styles

The same widgets that may be in a default state, for instance, a button, may also be in a hover state. Widgets enter a hover state when a user moves the mouse pointer over the widget. We want our user interface to give some kind of visual indication that the user has hovered over something they can click. It's time to give our theme some hover state styles:

1. Continuing with our theme design, expand the **Clickable: hover state** section.

2. In the **Background color & texture** section, click on the texture selector in the middle. Select the inset hard texture.

3. Change the **Border** color setting value to **#787878**.

4. Change the **Icon** color setting value to **#212121**:

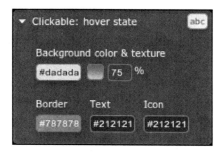

What just happened?

When we hover over widgets that support the hover state, their appearance is now harmonized with our theme settings. The background texture was updated to match the texture of the default state styles. The border color is now slightly darker. This makes the widget really stand out when the user hovers over it. At the same, it isn't so dark that it conflicts with the rest of the theme settings. Finally, we updated the icon color to match that of the font color.

Here is what the sample button widget looked like before we change the hover state settings:

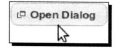

Here is what the sample button widget looked like after we updated the hover state theme settings:

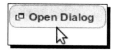

Time for action - setting active state styles

Some jQuery UI widgets, the same widgets that can be in either a default or hover state, can also be in an active state. Widgets become active after a user clicks them. For instance, the currently selected tab in a tabs widget is in an active state. We can control the appearance of active widgets through the ThemeRoller:

1. Continuing with our theme design, expand the **Clickable: active state** section.

2. In the **Background color & texture** section, change the color setting value on the left to **#f9f9f9**.

3. In the **Background color & texture** section, click the texture selector in the middle. Select the flat texture.

4. In the **Background color & texture** section, set the opacity setting value on the right-hand side to **100%**.

5. Change the **Border** color setting value to **#808080**.

6. Change the **Icon** color setting value to **#212121**:

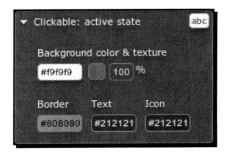

What just happened?

Widgets in the active state will now use our updated theme styles. We've changed the background color to something only marginally darker. The reason being, we are using the highlight soft texture in our content theme settings. This means that the color gets lighter toward the top. The color at the top is what we're aiming for in the active state styles. The texture has been changed to flat. Flat textures, unlike the others, have no pattern - they're simply a color. Accordingly, we've changed the background opacity to 100%. We do this because for these theme settings, we're only interested in showing the color.

The active state border is slightly darker, a visual cue to show that the widget is in fact active. Finally, like other adjustments we've made in our theme, the icon color now mirrors the text color.

Here is what the sample tabs widget looked like before we changed the active state theme settings:

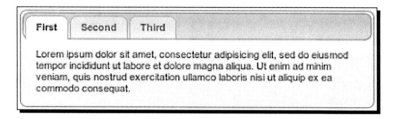

Here is what the sample tabs widget looks like after we've updated the active state theme settings.

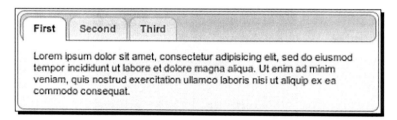

Notice that the selected tab's border stands out among the other tabs and how the selected tab blends better with the tab content.

Cues

In any web application, it is important to have the ability to notify users of events that have taken place. Perhaps an order was successfully processed, or a registration field was entered incorrectly. Both occurrences are worth letting the user know about. These are types of cues.

The jQuery UI theming framework defines two types of cues used to notify the user. These are highlights and errors. A highlight cue is informational, something that needs to be brought to the user's attention. An error is something exceptional that should not have happened.

Both cue categories can be customized to meet the requirements of any theme. It is important to keep in mind that cues are meant to aggressively grab the attention of the user - not to passively display information. So the theme styles applied to these elements really stand out. In this section we'll take a look at how to make this happen with the ThemeRoller.

Time for action - changing the highlight cue

A user of your jQuery UI application has just saved something. How do they know it was successful? Your application needs to inform them somehow—it needs to highlight the fact that something interesting just happened. To do this, your application will display a highlight cue. Let's add some highlight styles to our theme:

1. Continuing with our theme design, expand the **Highlight** section.

2. In the **Background color & texture** section, change the color setting value to **#faf2c7**.

3. In the **Background color & texture** section, change the opacity setting value to **85%**.

4. Change the **Border** color setting value to **#f8df49**.

5. Change the **Text** color setting value to **#212121**:

What just happened?

The theme settings for any highlight cues we display for the user have been updated. The background color is a shade darker and the opacity has been increased by 10%. The border color is now significantly darker than the background color. The contrast between the background and border colors defined here are now better aligned with the background-border contrast defined in other theme sections. Finally, we've updated the text color to be the same as the text in other sections. This is not for a noticeable difference (there isn't any), but for consistency reasons.

Here is what the sample highlight cue looked like before we updated the theme settings:

> ⓘ **Hey!** Sample ui-state-highlight style.

Here is what the sample highlight widget looks like after the theme setting changes:

Time for action - changing the error cue

Assume a user of your jQuery UI application has done something wrong, or perhaps the application has failed in one way or another. In both cases, you need to let your user know by displaying an error cue. Let's update our theme's error styles:

1. Continuing with our theme design, expand the **Error** section.

2. In the **Background color & texture** section, change the background color setting value to **#fad8d6**.

3. In the **Background color & texture** section, change the texture setting value to diagonals small.

4. In the **Background color & texture** section, change the opacity setting value to **85%**.

5. Change the **Border** color setting value to **#af0404**:

What just happened?

We've changed the appearance of any error messages displayed in a jQuery UI application that is using our theme. First, we updated the background color to be slightly darker. The background texture has been changed to use diagonal lines and the background opacity has been brought down to 85%. The diagonal lines help illustrate that there is a problem for the user. Finally, as with the rest of our custom theme, the border setting was set a shade darker so that it stands out better.

Here is what the error cue looked like before we changed the theme settings:

Here is what the error cue looks like after we changed the theme settings:

Overlays and shadows

There are special theme settings that allow us to specify how overlays used with dialog widgets look and how widgets with shadows look. Both of these themes are nonessential because they're seldom used. The dialog overlay exists mostly to set the opacity level of the user interface when a modal dialog is displayed. Shadows are only used if the developer uses the CSS classes explicitly.

We don't usually need to change these theme settings. The defaults are generally sufficient for basic use. Nonetheless, these sections are in the ThemeRoller application for when you do need them.

Time for action - dialog overlays

When a jQuery UI dialog is displayed, the user is focused on the dialog, not the rest of the user interface. Especially if the dialog is a modal - in which case an overlay is placed over the rest of the browser screen. We can change the way this overlay looks in the ThemeRoller:

1. Continuing with our theme design, expand the **Modal Screen for Overlays** section.

2. In the **Background color & texture** section, change the texture setting value to diagonals small.

3. In the **Background color & texture** section, change the opacity setting value to **50%**.

4. Change the **Overlay Opacity** setting value to **40%**:

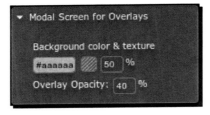

What just happened?

The background, behind modal dialogs will now display our theme updated theme changes. Similar to the error cue, we've updated the modal overlay texture to show dashed lines. This helps the user focus in on the dialog being displayed. We set the background opacity **50%**, which also helps hide the rest of the user interface while the dialog is displayed. The **Overlay Opacity** is set to **40%**. This is different from the background opacity in that it controls the opacity of the overlay as a whole, not just the background texture.

Here is what the sample dialog overlay looked like before we updated our theme settings:

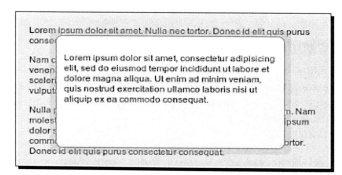

Here is what the sample dialog overlay looked like after we updated our theme settings:

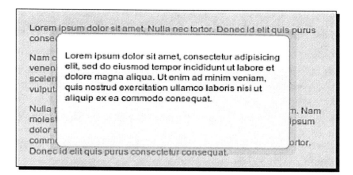

Time for action - defining shadows

Shadows can give a nice visual appeal to a widget. In fact, they can change the entire perspective of the user interface. This, amongst other shadow settings, can be controlled with the ThemeRoller:

1. Continuing with our theme design, expand the **Drop Shadows** section.

2. Change the **Shadow Opacity** setting value to **40%**.

3. Change the **Shadow Thickness** setting value to **4px**.

4. Change the **Top Offset** setting value to **0px**.

5. Change the **Left Offset** setting value to **0px**:

What just happened?

We've just change the orientation and thickness of shadows defined by our theme styles. We also made the shadow slightly darker by setting the opacity to **40%**. The shadow thickness was cut in half by setting it to **4px**. We changed the orientation of the shadow by setting the top and left offsets to **0px**. This means that the shadow isn't visible to the top or left-hand side of the element it is applied to, only the right-hand side and the bottom.

Here is what the sample shadow looked like before we updated the theme settings:

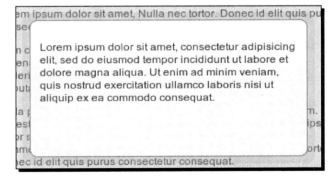

Here is what the sample shadow looks like after the theme settings are updated:

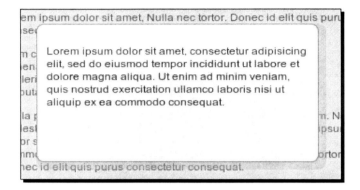

It looks as though the light is hitting the element from the user's top left-hand side.

Well, there you have it. Your first custom jQuery UI theme built entirely with the ThemeRoller. Here is the really long and *ugly* URL you can use to experiment with and edit the theme:

```
http://jqueryui.com/themeroller/#ffDefault=Lucida+Grande%2C+Lucida+Sa
ns%2C+Arial%2C+sans-serif&fwDefault=bold&fsDefault=1.1em&
cornerRadius=8px&bgColorHeader=cccccc&bgTextureHeader=06_inset
_hard.png&bgImgOpacityHeader=65&borderColorHeader=828282&fcHeader=222
222&iconColorHeader=222222&bgColorContent=f5f5f4&bgTexture
Content=03_highlight_soft.png&bgImgOpacityContent=75&borderColorConte
nt=828282&fcContent=222222&iconColorContent=222222&bgColorDefault=
e6e6e6&bgTextureDefault=06_inset_hard.png&bgImgOpacityDefault=65&bord
erColorDefault=b0b0b0&fcDefault=555555&iconColorDefault=555555&
bgColorHover=dadada&bgTextureHover=06_inset_hard.png&bgImgOpacity
Hover=75&borderColorHover=787878&fcHover=212121&iconColorHover=212121
&bgColorActive=f9f9f9&bgTextureActive=01_flat.png&bgImgOpacityActive=
100&borderColorActive=808080&fcActive=212121&iconColorActive=212121&
bgColorHighlight=faf2c7&bgTextureHighlight=02_glass.png&bgImgOpacity
Highlight=85&borderColorHighlight=f8df49&fcHighlight=212121&iconColor
Highlight=2e83ff&bgColorError=fad8d6&bgTextureError=07_diagonals_
small.png&bgImgOpacityError=85&borderColorError=af0404&fcError=cd0a
0a&iconColorError=cd0a0a&bgColorOverlay=aaaaaa&bgTextureOverlay=07_
diagonals_small.png&bgImgOpacityOverlay=50&opacityOverlay=40&bgColorS
hadow=aaaaaa&bgTextureShadow=01_flat.png&bgImgOpacityShadow=0&opacity
Shadow=40&thicknessShadow=4px&offsetTopShadow=0px&offsetLeftShadow=0p
x&cornerRadiusShadow=8px
```

Have a go hero

The URL we use to save our theme settings allows us to make further changes to our theme later on. Try saving the ThemeRoller URL to a local file and editing it later.

Changing existing themes

Up until now, we've selected themes from the theme gallery to use in our jQuery UI application and created our own theme from scratch. It would be nice if there was a way we could unite the two. Luckily, the ThemeRoller application lets us do just that. We can use an existing prepackaged theme as a starting point to create our own theme. Using this approach is similar to starting from scratch—we have all the mentioned theme settings at our disposal. The difference, and the big time saver, is that we should only have to make a few minor adjustments instead of mulling over each individual theme setting in fine detail.

You may have noticed beside the **Download** button for each theme in the gallery is an **Edit** button. We can use this button to take us to the roll your own theme tab. This will show us the settings for the selected theme.

In this section, we'll take an existing theme and update it for our needs.

Selecting a theme

Before we can use the ThemeRoller application to modify a prepackaged theme, we have to select one. This doesn't mean that we aimlessly choose the first theme we see. There should be a methodical process when deciding on a theme to edit. With the ThemeRoller application, we have the ability to see ahead of time what widgets will look like with a theme applied to them. These can be the sample widgets provided by ThemeRoller or our own widgets if you're building a theme using the dev tool. You'll want to look, in depth, at what the outcome of each theme setting change will be for each widget. If you skip over this step, chances are you'll end up finding something about your theme you don't like after you've built and downloaded it. Remember, the idea behind building on the work of prepackaged themes is to save time. Make sure you choose something that will aid in this.

Time for action - adjusting a theme

We've seen the role really long and ugly URLs play with the ThemeRoller. It is now time to use them to edit an existing theme:

1. Point your web browser to `http://jqueryui.com/themeroller/`.

2. Click on the **Edit** button on the **Start** theme.

3. Expand each section and experiment with different theme settings.

4. Bookmark the browser URL once you're happy with the changes:

What just happened?

We've selected a prepackaged jQuery UI theme as a basis for building our own. Clicking on the **Edit** button generated a long and ugly URL that took us to the roll your own theme section. The difference being, all the theme settings are populated with the styles that make up the Start theme:

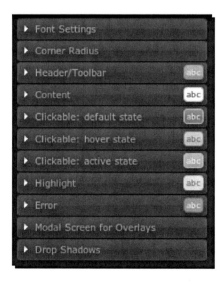

As we've seen in the previous sections of this chapter, you will more than likely leave some theme settings alone. If you're selecting a theme to edit, you'll probably only end up having to make minor adjustments.

Summary

We've learned a lot about the ThemeRoller application in this chapter. Theme authors can use this tool for just about any jQuery UI application. This is due mostly to the flexibility in the CSS framework itself. It is also largely due to the portability of ThemeRoller. We can access it from anywhere - it is a hosted application. We can use ThemeRoller from the jQuery UI website or we can use the dev tool - a compact version of ThemeRoller that allows us to develop themes using our own widgets.

The main idea behind the ThemeRoller is the design themes visually. To accomplish this, we need visual feedback whenever something is changed. This could be an individual theme property or a theme selection from the gallery. It is important that we see these changes applied to either the supplied sample widgets or our own widgets, depending on which version of ThemeRoller we're using. This immediate feedback plays a role in the development process of jQuery UI applications. There is no need to constantly build, download, deploy, and test.

Not only is there a huge theme selection in the gallery, but we can start building themes from the ground up, if we're so inclined. We have every theme setting at our fingertips with the ThemeRoller. And if we don't want to start from the ground up, we have the option of building on a prepackaged theme from the gallery.

Now that we've seen how to use the ThemeRoller to build our themes, we're ready to dig a little deeper into the underlying CSS.

In the next chapter, we'll take a look at the fundamental style constructs of jQuery UI themes—widget containers.

4

Working with Widget Containers

This chapter covers widget containers. Widget containers have the biggest impact on your theme, so this is a good starting point for fine-grained theme changes. This is much more fine-grained than the ThemeRoller we saw in the previous chapter.

In this chapter, we shall:

◆ Learn what widget containers are

◆ See how containers relate to widgets

◆ Explore the widget container CSS classes

So let's get on with it.

What are widget containers?

Every jQuery UI widget has a container element. This is the outer-most element in the nested HTML elements that make up the widget. For instance, this might be a `div` element. Inside the `div`, we find subordinate elements that give the widget its look and feel. Within the outer container element, widgets are sometimes further divided into sub-containers. Widgets can have header elements as well as main content elements.

What do widget containers have to do with themes? Widget containers are used to apply the most general theme style properties to widgets. This includes things such as fonts, borders, and background colors. The container HTML elements are given container CSS classes from the jQuery UI theme framework.

Containers and widgets

The following is an example of how the jQuery UI tabs widget uses container elements to apply container CSS classes from the theming framework:

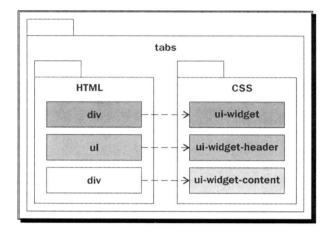

Here we can see how the HTML elements of the tabs widget relate to the CSS classes of the theming framework. The first HTML `div` element is the outer container of the tabs widget and has the `ui-widget` CSS class applied to it. The `ul` HTML element defines the header of the tabs widget. The header contains the individual tabs. The tab's `ul` header element has a `ui-widget-header` CSS class applied to it. Finally, the last `div` HTML element contains the selected tab content and has a `ui-widget-content` CSS class applied to it.

These three CSS classes are the containers of the jQuery UI theming framework. We'll spend the rest of this chapter divulging the details of these theme classes.

The ui-widget class

As we've seen in the previous section, the `ui-widget` class is applied to all jQuery UI widgets at the outer-most layer. The styles defined by this class are applied to widget elements in a cascading fashion (like any CSS class applied to an outer HTML element) until they're overridden by other styles.

The `ui-widget` class defines font settings for all our jQuery UI widgets. We've actually seen this in action in the previous chapter. The ThemeRoller application—used to build custom jQuery UI themes - allows us to define font style properties. These changes affect every widget. This consistent property of jQuery UI themes is made possible by the `ui-widget` class.

Now that we understand, a little better, the role of the `ui-widget` class, it's time to take a deeper look at the underlying CSS.

Time for action - preparing the example

Here, we're going to set up an example that we can reuse throughout the chapter:

1. If you haven't already, download and extract the jQuery UI package into a directory called `jqueryui` from `http://jqueryui.com/download`.

2. At the same level as the `jqueryui` directory, create a new `index.html` file with the following content:

```
<html xmlns="http://www.w3.org/1999/xhtml">

  <head>

    <title>Working With Widget Containers</title>

    <link href="jqueryui/development-
    bundle/themes/base/jquery.ui.all.css" rel="stylesheet"
    type="text/css" />

  </head>

  <body style="font-size: 10px;">

    <div class="ui-widget">My Widget Container</div>

  </body>

</html>
```

3. Open `index.html` in a web browser. You should see something similar to the following:

My Widget Container

What just happened?

We've created a simple HTML file that we'll use throughout the rest of the chapter. The first thing you'll notice that is different about this HTML file is the path we're using to include the theme CSS. We're pointing to the development-bundle instead of CSS in the path. Additionally, instead of importing a CSS file with a name such as `jquery-ui-version-custom.css`, we're importing `jquery.ui.all.css`.

There are a couple of reasons for this. First, we want to reference files in the `development-bundle` directory because this isn't production CSS we're working with. We'll be modifying individual CSS style properties manually. Second, the `development-bundle` directory separates different parts of the theme framework into different CSS files. This comes in handy when we have to get our hands dirty with CSS.

In the body of our HTML file, we've added a single `div` element that contains some text. We've applied the `ui-widget` CSS class to this element. All that will have changed in appearance by applying this class is the font styles. However, the idea here isn't the HTML output as much as preparing for the following sections.

Widget fonts

Using the ThemeRoller application allows us to set the font settings for our custom theme. We can set the font weight, font size, and font family properties here. There are, however, some limitations to setting your theme font settings using the *ThemeRoller* application. For instance, you can only set the font weight to normal or bold. For more fine-grained changes to things like this, we need to alter the CSS manually.

Time for action - changing widget fonts

Let's update the `ui-widget` font style properties:

1. In the `jqueryui/development-bundle/themes/base` directory, edit the `jquery.ui.theme.css` file.

2. Locate the `.ui-widget` style definition; it should be near the top of the section labeled component containers.

3. Replace the `.ui-widget` style definition with the following:

```
.ui-widget {
    font-family: Verdana,Arial,sans-serif;
    font-size: 1.1em;
    font-weight: 900;

}
```

4. Reload `index.html` in your web browser. You should see something similar to the following:

My Widget Container

What just happened?

We've added a new style property to the `ui-widget` class - font-weight. We've set the value of this property to `900`. This will give elements with the `ui-widget` class applied to it, in our case a `div` element, a bold font. We could have just used the theme roller to set the `font-weight` property to bold and gotten the same effect. However, the point here is to illustrate that you have the same flexibility as you do with any other CSS project. Maybe your design team prefers to use integer values and is more comfortable with using this notation. There is nothing in the jQuery UI theming standards that stops them from doing so.

Have a go hero

Try experimenting with setting the font size in the `ui-widget` class using percentage values and pixel values. What other font settings can be set here? Try using the font-variant property here. Does it have the effect you've anticipated?

Scaling widget fonts

You'll notice that when designing themes using the ThemeRoller, the font size setting defaults to using the em unit. For example, 1em=16px. This is the default font size in all web browsers. So, if we were to set the font size of all our widgets to 1.1em, the size of our font in pixels would be 17.6.

Using the em size unit is the recommended way to size fonts using CSS. This is due to the fact that it works consistently in all web browsers. The alternative is to set our widget font size using pixel or percentage values. Again, the problem being that we want our application to look consistent across all browser platforms and we're defining the font size as part of our theme. So we need to use the best CSS tools available to us.

Using the em font size unit poses an interesting problem with regard to jQuery UI widget containers. What would happen to the font size if we were to place a widget container inside another widget container? If our theme uses a global font size of 1.1em, it means that every element with a `ui-widget` class will be slightly larger than its parent element's font size. This means that every nested element with a `ui-widget` class and a parent with a `ui-widget` class will grow in font size!

To deal with this tricky scenario, the theming CSS framework provides a style definition for this exact purpose. The `.ui-widget .ui-widget` style definition resets the font size to it's parent font size so that we avoid the infinite growth of font size. We can also use this style to our advantage should we decide we want to change the way the widget `font-size` scales with regard to sub-containers.

Time for action - scaling down font size

Rather than have font sizes stay the same as their parent containers, let's assume we want them to shrink or scale down. We can take care of this behavior in the theme CSS:

1. Open the `index.html` file created earlier and replace the content with the following:

```
<html xmlns="http://www.w3.org/1999/xhtml">

  <head>

    <title>Working With Widget Containers</title>

    <link href="jqueryui/development-
    bundle/themes/base/jquery.ui.all.css"  rel="stylesheet"
    type="text/css" />

  </head>

  <body style="font-size: 100%;">

    <div class="ui-widget">My Widget Container</div>

      <div class="ui-widget">
        <div class="ui-widget">My Contained Widget</div>
      </div>

    </div>

  </body>

</html>
```

2. In the `jqueryui/development-bundle/themes/base` directory, edit the `jquery.ui.theme.css` file.

3. Locate the `.ui-widget .ui-widget` style definition and replace it with the following:

```
.ui-widget .ui-widget {

  font-size: 0.9em;

}
```

4. Reload `index.html` in your web browser. You should see something like this:

> My Widget Container
> My Contained Widget

What just happened?

In `index.html`, we've created a new container `div` with the `ui-widget` CSS class applied to it. The first container `div` we created in the previous example remains unchanged. This new container has something new—a sub-container. This is simply a `div` with the `ui-widget` class applied to it. This HTML structure matches the style definition we edited in `jquery.ui.theme.css` - `.ui-widget` `.ui-widget`. As you can see, this results in the `0.9em` font size being applied to the contained element and the font size scaling down to 15.83 pixels. The following figure illustrates how the font size changes with nested elements that have the `ui-widget` class applied to them:

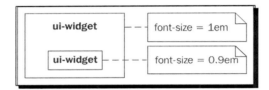

Have a go hero

Change the `font-size` style property of the `.ui-widget` `.ui-widget` style definition back to `1em`. Create three or more levels of nested `ui-widget` container elements. Does the `.ui-widget` `.ui-widget` style prevent the font size from shrinking at each level?

Widget form fields

Widget containers, elements with a `ui-widget` CSS class applied to them, can also contain form fields. These include text inputs, submit buttons, and selectors. How do the styles of the `ui-widget` class impact the appearance of child form elements? Remember, the `ui-widget` class is responsible for giving widgets their font styles. But the form elements don't inherit those font styles from the parent. Instead, they inherit form styles from the operating system or from the web browser.

This is addressed in the jQuery UI theming framework by defining a style specifically for form elements within a container element that has a `ui-widget` class applied to it.

Time for action - changing widget form fields

It's time to add a form element to our sample container and adjust the font settings:

1. Open the `index.html` file created earlier and replace the content with the following:

```
<html xmlns="http://www.w3.org/1999/xhtml">

  <head>

    <title>Working With Widget Containers</title>

      <link href="jqueryui/development-
      bundle/themes/base/jquery.ui.all.css" rel="stylesheet"
      type="text/css" />

  </head>

  <body style="font-size: 100%;">

    <div class="ui-widget">

      <label>Type Something:</label>
      <input type="text"/>

    </div>

  </body>

</html>
```

2. In the `jqueryui/development-bundle/themes/base` **directory, edit the** `jquery.ui.theme.css` **file.**

3. Locate the `.ui-widget input, .ui-widget select, .ui-widget textarea, .ui-widget button` style definition and replace it with the following:

```
.ui-widget input, .ui-widget select, .ui-widget textarea, .ui-
widget button {

    font-family: Courier New,Arial,sans-serif;
    font-size: 0.9em;

}
```

4. Reload `index.html` in your web browser. You should see something similar to the following:

Type Something: `Something`

What just happened?

We've added a new `input` element to our sample `div`. We also added a label to the left-hand side of the input that describes what the `input` is for.

In `jquery.ui.theme.css`, we updated the style definition of form elements within containers. We changed the primary font-family to courier new. We also changed the font size from `1em` to `0.9em`. The font size change is the same as in the previous section.

You probably noticed that before we made these changes, the style definition for form elements in an element with a `ui-widget` class are the same as those of the main `.ui-widget` style. In fact, you can see that the label we added beside the `input` inherits these font styles from the parent `div`. Remember, the `ui-widget` class is used to apply theme font settings to all widgets. This includes widgets that have form elements as children.

As form elements don't inherit the font settings of the parent, this form element style definition is necessary in order to apply the `ui-widget` CSS class to elements and see a consistent result. For instance, the following figure illustrates how the `font-family` style property would be applied to form elements within a `ui-widget` container by the theme framework:

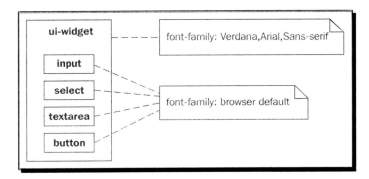

Instead of leaving the font settings to use the default, the `ui-widget` class overrides this, using theme font settings. Our theme now uses a specific `font-family` for form elements and scales down the font size. The following figure illustrates how the form elements style definition consistently applies the `font-family` property to contained form elements:

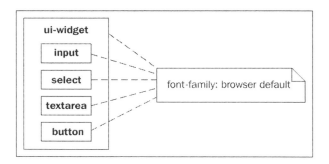

Sometimes, it may be tempting to expand your theme by adding new style properties to the `ui-widget class`. This is fine to get around a specific problem, or to experiment with a new theme. Keep in mind, however, that the `ui-widget` class is applied to every jQuery UI widget and should be kept as general as possible.

Have a go hero

By default, the same styles are defined in the `ui-widget` form elements style as those in the `.ui-widget` class. Rather than have an exact duplicate set of style properties, is there a better way to do this? Or is this redundancy a fact we have to deal with?

Pop quiz - the ui-widget class

1. Which jQuery UI widgets is the ui-widget class applied to?

    a. The `ui-widget` class is applied to all jQuery UI widgets.

    b. The `ui-widget` class is applied only to top-level widgets.

    c. User interface designers need to manually apply the `ui-widget` class to HTML elements.

2. Why does the `ui-widget` class set font sizes in `em` units?

    a. The `em` size unit implicitly scales to the size of the parent element. It is easier for theme authors to work with factors, for example, 1.1, instead of percentages, like 17%. The `em` unit is also more reliable across web browsers.

b.   The em size unit is more efficient than percentages or pixel units.

c.   The em size unit is more accurate than percentages of pixel units

3.   What don't form elements inherit from a parent `ui-widget` container?

a.   Form elements don't inherit font settings from their parent containers. This is why they're defined explicitly in jQuery UI themes.

b.   Form elements aren't part of themes.

c.   Form elements cannot change font styles by using CSS alone.

The ui-widget-content class

The `ui-widget` class is at the top of the CSS class hierarchy that makes up the jQuery UI theming framework. We've seen how it is applied to top-level HTML elements as well as the child elements inside parent widget containers. Widgets aren't just containers—they must have content that gives them real meaning as well. Just as we use the `ui-widget` class to consistently apply font styles, we use the `ui-widget-content` class to refine core elements of a widget.

Content borders

The `ui-widget-content` class gives the content of jQuery UI widgets their borders. This includes things such as the color and thickness. Both of these border style attributes can be set in the ThemeRoller application when designing your theme. The result generated by the ThemeRoller is placed in the `ui-widget-content` CSS class. We can directly manipulate the CSS to further customize the widget content border styles in ways we cannot with the ThemeRoller alone.

Time for action - styling content borders

It's time to add additional styles to the widget content borders of our theme. We'll add an outset property to give the appearance of a three-dimensional widget:

1.   Open the `index.html` file created earlier and replace the content with the following:

```
<html xmlns="http://www.w3.org/1999/xhtml">

  <head>

    <title>Working With Widget Containers</title>

    <link href="jqueryui/development-bundle/themes/base/jquery.
ui.all.css" rel="stylesheet" type="text/css" />
```

```
    </head>
    <body>
      <div class="ui-widget ui-widget-content" style="width: 20%;">
        <div>My Widget Border</div>
      </div>
    </body>
</html>
```

2. In the `jqueryui/development-bundle/themes/base` directory, edit the `jquery.ui.theme.css` file.

3. Locate the `.ui-widget-content` style definition and replace it with the following:

```
.ui-widget-content {
    border: 3px outset #aaaaaa;
    background: #ffffff url(images/ui-
    bg_flat_75_ffffff_40x100.png) 50% 50% repeat-x;
    color: #222222;
}
```

4. Reload `index.html` in your web browser. You should see something similar to the following screenshot:

What just happened?

We've created an HTML `div` element with two classes—`ui-widget` and `ui-widget-content`. This is an element that is a widget and has widget content; the content in this case being a nested `div` element. The `ui-widget` class gives the element its font settings while the `ui-widget-content` class defines the font color, the background color, and the border. The following figure illustrates which style properties are applied by which CSS class:

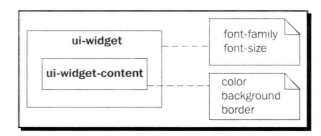

We've also given an inline style to the outer `div` that sets the width to `20%`. This is only to prevent `div` from occupying the entire width of the page and isn't relevant to the example.

In `jquery.ui.theme.css`, we changed the width of the border to 3px. We also changed the border type from `solid` to `outset` which gives a 3-dimensional appearance. There are several other CSS border styles to choose from, although the important thing to note here is that we've updated the border styles for all widget types that have a `ui-widget-content` class.

Have a go hero

Experiment with different `border-style` values. Which ones add value to the theme's overall appeal and which ones don't?

Time for action - border sides

In the previous example, we changed the appearance of the entire `ui-widget-content` border. In the theme CSS, we can also apply border styles to specific sides should we choose to do so:

1. In the `jqueryui/development-bundle/themes/base` directory, edit the `jquery.ui.theme.css` file.

2. Locate the `.ui-widget-content` style definition and replace it with the following:

```
.ui-widget-content {

    border: 1px solid #aaaaaa;
    border-bottom-width: 2px;
    background: #ffffff url(images/ui-bg_flat_75_ffffff_40x100.
    png)
    50% 50% repeat-x;
    color: #222222;

}
```

3. Reload `index.html` in your web browser. You should see something similar to the following:

```
My Widget Border
```

What just happened?

We've reused the same HTML in `index.html` from the previous example. We have a `div` element with `ui-widget` and `ui-widget-content` CSS classes applied to it.

In `jquery.ui.theme.css`, we've added a new border CSS property to the `ui-widget-content` class—`border-bottom-width`. We use this property to set the bottom border width of our container to `2px`. The remaining sides of the border get their width, `1px`, from the border CSS property. The following figure illustrates how the individual border sides are applied to the container via the `ui-widget-content` class:

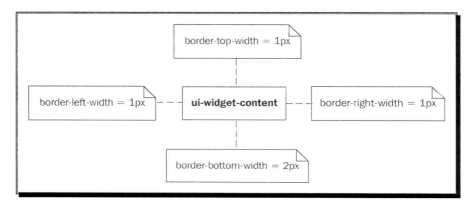

What we've done is overridden an aspect of the theme. This is different from changing the value of a style property. For instance, in the previous example we changed the border type to `outset`. This is simply a CSS property value. By adding the `border-bottom-width` property, we've added a new dimension to our theme; something that can be configured independently from other theme properties.

Have a go hero

Try setting other properties of individual border sides. For instance, can we set the left-hand side border color and style in our theme? When, if ever, would it make sense to do this?

Content links

Within `ui-widget-content` elements, we may have link elements. Links signify to the user that this is something that may be clicked. We can use the theme CSS to change the appearance of links within widget content elements. This includes the color of text links that are, by default, set to the same color as the font when designing themes using the ThemeRoller.

Time for action - changing link colors

It's time to update the color of links within widgets for our theme. This is easy to achieve with simple CSS modifications:

1. Open the `index.html` file created earlier and replace the content with the following:

```
<html xmlns="http://www.w3.org/1999/xhtml">

  <head>

    <title>Working With Widget Containers</title>

        <link href="jqueryui/development-
        bundle/themes/base/jquery.ui.all.css" rel="stylesheet"
        type="text/css" />

  </head>

  <body style="font-size: 100%;">

    <div class="ui-widget ui-widget-content" style="width:20%;">
      <a href="#">Click Me</a>

    </div>

  </body>

</html>
```

2. In the `jqueryui/development-bundle/themes/base` directory, edit the `jquery.ui.theme.css` file.

3. Locate the `.ui-widget-content` a style definition and replace it with the following:

```
.ui-widget-content a {

    color: #12153b;
    font-size: 0.9em;

}
```

4. Reload `index.html` in your web browser. You should see something similar to the following:

Click Me

What just happened?

We've created a new link element that lives in the widget content. This link is now subjected to styles defined in the ui-widget-content CSS class.

In jquery.ui.theme.css, we've changed the theme styles for links that are displayed inside elements with the ui-widget-content class applied to it. The link text color has been changed to #12153b. We've also changed the link font size as we have in previous sections to 0.9em.

Before we made these changes to the .ui-widget-content a style definition, you probably noticed that the link color property was set to the same as the font color defined in the ui-widget CSS class. The same approach as with form elements is used for link elements. Recall that form elements do not inherit font style properties from their parent element. Likewise, the link we've created here doesn't inherit the color property from its parent div. The following figure illustrates how link elements within ui-widget-content containers acquire their color style property if not for the .ui-widget-content a style definition. Even though the color is defined in the parent container, the link doesn't inherit it.

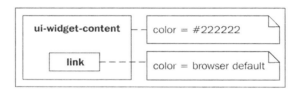

The jQuery UI theming framework uses this overriding approach to make links placed inside widget content look consistent by implementing the .ui-widget-content a style definition. The following is an illustration of how links share the font color defined in the parent container.

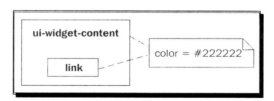

Otherwise, we'd see the default appearance the browser uses for links. This is usually a light blue for unvisited links and purple for visited links. With themeable user interfaces, we don't want the browser deciding how elements change their appearance.

Have a go hero

Try letting the link elements inside `ui-widget-content` containers use the browser default styles. Hint: remove the `ui-widget-content a` style definition from the theme.

Pop quiz – the ui-widget-content class

1. What types of elements belong in `ui-widget-content` containers?

    a. Any HTML elements that make up the core of the widget.

    b. The widget header.

    c. Only `div` HTML elements.

2. What can we do in the `ui-widget-content` class with borders that we cannot do in the ThemeRoller?

    a. The ThemeRoller only sets the border color. So anything else, including border styles, width, customizing individual sides, needs to be implemented manually in the `ui-widget-content` CSS.

    b. Widget borders cannot be altered by manually editing the `ui-widget-content` class.

    c. The border width.

3. Why do link elements have a style definition in `ui-widget-content` containers?

    a. By default, links do not inherit the color of their parent container. This is explicitly defined in the theming framework.

    b. To support multiple web browsers.

    c. To prevent changes from being made to links outside of the theme.

The ui-widget-header class

CSS styles for widgets includes the overall widget container itself using the `ui-widget` class and the inside of the widget where the widget components can be found. This is done with the `ui-widget-content` class. The final widget container class is `ui-widget-header`. As the name suggests, widget headers usually indicate to the user what the widget is. Within the jQuery UI theming framework, we have several options available to us for customizing the appearance of widget headers.

Header borders

If you take a look at the sections for widget content and widget headers in the ThemeRoller, you'll notice that they're similar. All style properties we can set for widget content may also be set for widget headers. This doesn't mean that they should be identical, but it highlights the fact that the two are consistent with one another. This is confirmed by looking at the CSS for the two classes—they share the same style properties.

Just like widget content, widget headers have borders we can customize. Also, like widget content borders, we can set style properties for them in the ThemeRoller and there are some aspects we want to control directly in the CSS. Widget header borders also have to consider the borders around them. That is, widget headers exist inside a widget that has a border. So the theme designer will take care to not contradict the two border styles.

Time for action - Styling header borders

It's time to create a widget header element and give its borders some styles in the theming framework CSS:

1. Open the `index.html` file created earlier and replace the content with the following:

```html
<html xmlns="http://www.w3.org/1999/xhtml">

  <head>

    <title>Working With Widget Containers</title>

    <link href="jqueryui/development-
    bundle/themes/base/jquery.ui.all.css" rel="stylesheet"
    type="text/css" />

  </head>

  <body style="font-size: 100%;">

    <div class="ui-widget ui-widget-content" style="width:20%;">

      <h2 class="ui-widget-header">My Header</h2>
      <div>My Content</div>

    </div>

  </body>

</html>
```

2. In the `jquery/development-bundle/themes/base` **directory, edit** `jquery.ui.theme.css`.

3. Locate the `.ui-widget-header` style definition and replace it with the following:

```
.ui-widget-header {

    border: 2px inset #aaaaaa;
    background: #cccccc url(images/ui-bg_highlight-
    soft_75_cccccc_1x100.png) 50% 50% repeat-x;
    color: #222222;
    font-weight: bold;

}
```

4. Reload `index.html` in your web browser. You should see something similar to the following:

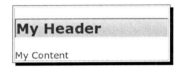

What just happened?

We've added a new header element to our widget `div`. The header is an `h2` element with a `ui-widget-header` class applied to it. You'll notice that the `h2` element is actually located within the `ui-widget-container`. Oddly enough, this means that styles from `ui-widget-content` will be applied to the header element as well. Aren't the header and and the remaining widget elements supposed to be styled independently? Remember, both `ui-widget-content` and `ui-widget-header` classes share the same style properties by default. So if we were to change the font color, say, in the `ui-widget-content` class, the font color defined in the `ui-widget-header` class would override this. Regardless, theme authors need to exercise caution when changes are manually made to both of these classes.

We can see in the following illustration how our header container overrides the border settings of the content container:

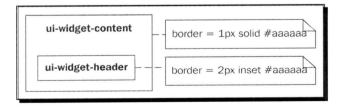

Time for action - border sides

If `ui-widget-content` elements can apply specific border styles to individual border sides, `ui-widget-header` elements must also be able to do so. Let's see how we can make distinct border alterations to widget header elements:

1. In the `jqueryui/development-bundle/themes/base` directory, edit `jquery.ui.theme.css`.

2. Locate the `.ui-widget-header` style definition and replace it with the following:

```
.ui-widget-header {
    border: 1px solid #aaaaaa;
    border-left-width: 0;
    border-right-width: 0;
    background: #cccccc url(images/ui-bg_highlight-
    soft_75_cccccc_1x100.png) 50% 50% repeat-x;
    color: #222222;
    font-weight: bold;
}
```

3. Reload `index.html` in your web browser. You should see something similar to the following:

What just happened?

Here, we're reusing the same `index.html` content from the previous section. We have a basic widget header and some basic widget content.

In `jquery.ui.theme.css`, we've made some border changes to the `ui-widget-header` class. The class now has two new border style properties - `border-left-width` and `border-right-width`. Both of these properties have a value of `0`, which hides those sides of the border entirely.

The reason we're doing this is to better match the header border with that of the widget content border. Before we made this change, the border of the widget header on both the left and right was the same width as the widget content - `1px`. What this did was make the left and right borders appear to be `2px` because both classes have borders associated with them. We don't want a width that has a border width of `1px` all around except for to the left and right of the header. This problem with the `ui-widget-header` class is illustrated as follows:

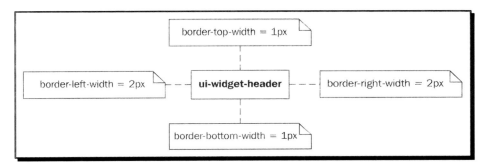

Removing these borders in the theming framework CSS addresses this issue for us as is illustrated as follows:

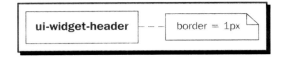

Have a go hero

Is this the best or only way to remove excess border space to the left-hand side and the right-hand side of widget header containers? Try to think of an alternative approach.

Header links

In addition to links appearing in widget content containers, links may also appear in headers. This might seem counter-intuitive at first; headers are supposed to identify the widget, and announce to the user why it is there. There is no reason widget headers cannot contain links that are central to the function of the widget.

By placing links in a widget header container, you're stating that we should pay close attention to these links. With the jQuery UI CSS framework, we can control how links displayed here look.

Time for action - header links

It's time to define a custom style for header links in our jQuery UI theme:

1. Open the `index.html` file created earlier and replace the content with the following:

```
<html xmlns="http://www.w3.org/1999/xhtml">

  <head>

    <title>Working With Widget Containers</title>

    <link href="jqueryui/development-
    bundle/themes/base/jquery.ui.all.css" rel="stylesheet"
    type="text/css" />

  </head>

    <body style="font-size: 100%;">

        <div class="ui-widget ui-widget-content"
          style="width:20%;">

            <div class="ui-widget-header">

                <a href="#" style="float: left;">prev</a>
                <a href="#" style="float: right;">next</a>
                <div style="text-align: center;">My Header</div>

            </div>

            <div style="clear: both;"></div>

            <div>My Content</div>

        </div>

    </body>

</html>
```

2. In the `jqueryui/development-bundle/themes/base` directory, edit the `jquery.ui.theme.css` file.

3. Locate the `.ui-widget-header a` style definition and replace it with the following:

```
.ui-widget-header a {

    color: #222222;
    font-size: 0.9em;
    font-weight: normal;
```

```
    }

    .ui-widget-header a:hover {

        color: #212121;
        text-decoration: none;

    }
```

4.   Reload `index.html` in your web browser. You should see something similar to the following:

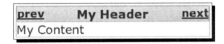

What just happened?

We've added two link elements to our widget header container. These are navigational links placed to the left-hand side and the right-hand side of the header text. This is done by placing in-line styles in the link elements. As we use the `float` style property to align the links in the header, we need to add a new `div` element that clears the alignment before the content widget container. To do this, we give the new `div` a `clear: both` in-line style.

 Keep in mind that in-line styles are only used here to format the example and should always be avoided in practice.

In `jquery.ui.theme.css`, we've updated the styles for links that are placed in widget header containers. We've kept the link `color` as the default but the font size is now smaller and the font weight is normal, down from bold. Additionally, we've created a new style definition—one that changes the appearance of links in header container widgets when the user hovers over them. This style changes the link color and removes the text decoration.

You'll notice that the header title stands out more than the links. This is due to the font weight being reduced to normal, while the header title remains bold. But at the same time, when looking at this widget, we're still drawn to the links; much more so than the actual content.

The jQuery UI theming framework has utilities for putting widgets into a hover state and thus changes their appearance accordingly. We're not interested in this here because it's not a widget that changes state when a user hovers over it, it's a component of the widget. Having said that, we're still in good shape if we want to use the hover class in our CSS selector.

Have a go hero

Can you think of any other use cases for links in a header container? Try building something links that stand out in the same way but aren't actually nested in the header container.

Pop quiz - the ui-widget-header class

1. Where does the `ui-widget-header` class belong in widget elements?

    a. The `ui-widget-header` class belongs in the `ui-widget-content` container.

    b. The `ui-widget-header` class doesn't belong in widget elements.

    c. The `ui-widget-header` class is always the first element found in widgets.

2. What is the difference between properties defined in the `ui-widget-header` class and those defined in the `ui-widget-content` class?

    a. Both classes define the same style properties.

    b. The `ui-widget-header` class only defines properties used for header elements.

    c. The `ui-widget-header` class doesn't define any font properties.

Summary

In this chapter, we've introduced a few important CSS classes involved with the jQuery UI theming framework. These three classes are applied to widget HTML elements to modify their look and feel. When we use the ThemeRoller application to assist in building our theme, the font, content, and header sections correlate to these CSS classes.

By their very nature, these classes are hierarchical. That is, `ui-widget` is to at the top-most level and is applied to every widget. This class defines the font settings for all jQuery UI applications.

The `ui-widget-content` class is just as important as the `ui-widget` class—it gives widgets general settings such as color, background, and borders.

Finally, the `ui-widget-header` class is used as a container to display the widget titles. We can also put other things in this container such as links.

Now that we've got a basic understanding of how the basic building blocks of the jQuery UI theming CSS framework work, it's time to extend these same principles into interactions states.

5
Transforming Interaction States

Interactions change the state of a user interface. The jQuery UI theming framework helps in representing these changes in state. As we've seen, widgets derive much of their look and feel from their containers and their CSS classes. Interaction states help give the user feedback while remaining in the boundaries of the theme.

In this chapter, we shall:

◆ Explore the interaction state CSS classes

◆ Relate these classes to different widgets

◆ Walk-through changing each class

So let's get on with it.

What are interaction states?

Users interact with jQuery UI widgets. This is usually with the mouse—they can click on a widget, hover over a widget, or they can drag the handles on a slider widget. The keyboard can also be used to interact with widgets—users can hit the *Tab* key to navigate around the application, resulting in a different widget having the focus. When a user does these things, interacts with widgets, the widgets change state. These are the interaction states of the jQuery UI theming framework.

When a widget enters a different interaction state, because the user hovered over the widget with the mouse for instance, the appearance is changed. This is a common behavior for most web applications—a user is notified visually that they've moved the mouse over something interesting. The difference with jQuery UI widgets is that these changes in state don't arbitrarily change the look of the widget. The visual changes associated with an interaction state are applied to the widget by a CSS class from the theming framework. There are a limited number of interaction states supported by the framework that may be applied to widgets. The interaction state classes and how they're used with jQuery UI widgets is the subject of this chapter.

Time for action - preparing the example

Its time to set up an example environment that we can use throughout the remainder of the chapter. This is the same idea as the previous chapter. However, if you walked through the examples in the previous chapter, should start with a new copy of the theme CSS files here. The changes made in the previous chapter might interfere with what we're trying to illustrate here:

1. If you haven't already, download and extract the jQuery UI package into a directory called `jqueryui` from `http://jqueryui.com/download`.

2. At the same level as the `jqueryui` directory, create a new `index.html` file with the following content:

```
<html xmlns="http://www.w3.org/1999/xhtml">

    <head>

        <title>Transforming Interaction States</title>

        <link href="jqueryui/development-bundle/themes/base/
          jquery.ui.all.css" rel="stylesheet" type="text/css" />

        <script src="jqueryui/js/jquery-1.5.x.min.js" type="text/
          javascript"></script>
        <script src="jqueryui/js/jquery-ui-1.8.x.custom.min.js"
          type="text/javascript"></script>
        <script src="index.js" type="text/javascript"></script>

    </head>

    <body style="font-size: 10px;">

        <button id="my_button">Click Me</button>
```

```
    </body>

</html>
```

3. At the same level as the jqueryui directory, create a new index.js file with the following content:

```
$(document).ready(function(){

    $("#my_button").button();

});
```

4. Open index.html in your web browser. You should see something similar to the following:

What just happened?

We've set up our example environment that we can use throughout the remainder of the chapter. In index.html, we've included the theme CSS as we did in the previous chapter, allowing us to modify our theme styles. The index.html file also includes three JavaScript files. The first is the jQuery core library, which is always required. The second is the jQuery UI JavaScript library, which defines all the default widgets. Finally, we've included our own index.js file where we create the jQuery UI widgets in our example. In the body of index.html, we have a simple button element with the ID my_button. This is used to create a jQuery UI button widget.

In index.js, we have a callback function that is executed when the page has finished loading in the web browser. Here, we take the my_button element and turn it into a jQuery UI button widget. We're only doing this to make sure our example is set up correctly. If the button looks good, we're ready to move on.

The default state

Widgets the user interacts with must have an initial state. That is, before the user does anything with the mouse or keyboard that would cause the widget to change state, it should look normal, as though nothing has happened to it yet. This is the default state. The default state has a corresponding CSS class within the theming framework that is applied to widgets. You're probably wondering why we don't use the ancestor styles from the framework to show the user that the widget is in a default state. Why do we need a another class applied to widgets the user interacts with?

jQuery UI widgets capable of user interaction need the default state because they may not necessarily inherit theme styles from container widgets such as `ui-widget-content`. It is a good thing that we want button widgets to look enticing, like they're supposed to be clicked. If we were to let our clickable widgets inherit container theme styles, they would fade into the background as an afterthought.

The default state is also important from a more elusive design perspective. If widgets change state when a user interacts with them, they get a new state applied to them. If not for the default state, the widget would be going from being a stateless entity to suddenly having a state. This doesn't make much sense logically. It is better that widgets with the potential to change state are always in one state or another, never stateless.

Default state selectors

In the previous chapter, we looked at widget container CSS classes. These CSS selectors were fairly straightforward - "any element with this class" or "any input elements nested inside an element with this class". Just like widget containers, the jQuery UI theming framework uses classes for states. The default state is called `ui-state-default`. The selectors used by this state are a little more involved than the widget container CSS selectors. Not only do we have nested elements that the default state affects, we also have groups of selectors required to make the default state behave as it's supposed to.

The default state selector isn't necessarily difficult to work with because it uses nesting and grouping selectors - it just has more moving parts than selectors in other areas of the CSS framework such as widget containers. In fact, the widget container classes are closely related to the default state class. The default state uses the `ui-widget-content` and `ui-widget-header` classes in its CSS selector.

Time for action - default container selectors

It's time to see the default state CSS selectors in action:

1. Edit the `index.html` file created earlier and replace the content with the following:

    ```
    <html xmlns="http://www.w3.org/1999/xhtml">

      <head>

        <title>Transforming Interaction States</title>

        <link href="jqueryui/development-
        bundle/themes/base/jquery.ui.all.css" rel="stylesheet"
        type="text/css" />
    ```

```
        <script src="jqueryui/js/jquery-1.5.x.min.js"
        type="text/javascript"></script>
        <script src="jqueryui/js/jquery-ui-1.8.x.custom.min.js"
        type="text/javascript"></script>
        <script src="index.js" type="text/javascript"></script>

    </head>

    <body style="font-size: 10px;">

      <div id="my_tabs" style="width: 40%;">

        <ul>
          <li><a href="#first">First</a></li>
          <li><a href="#second">Second</a></li>
          <li><a href="#third">Third</a></li>
        </ul>

        <div id="first">
          <p>First paragraph</p>
          <p>Second paragraph</p>
          <p>Third paragraph</p>
        </div>

        <div id="second">
          <p>First paragraph</p>
          <p>Second paragraph</p>
          <p>Third paragraph</p>
        </div>

        <div id="third">
          <p>First paragraph</p>
          <p>Second paragraph</p>
          <p>Third paragraph</p>
        </div>

      </div>

    </body>

</html>
```

2. Edit the `index.js` file created earlier and replace the content with the following:

```
$(document).ready(function(){

    $("#my_tabs").tabs();
});
```

3. In the `jqueryui/development-bundle/themes/base` directory, edit the `jquery.ui.theme.css` file.

4. Locate the `.ui-state-default, .ui-widget-content .ui-state-default, .ui-widget-header .ui-state-default` style definition and replace it with the following:

```
.ui-state-default {

    border: 1px solid #d3d3d3;
    background: #e6e6e6 url(images/ui-bg_glass_75_e6e6e6_1x400.
    png) 50% 50% repeat-x;
    font-weight: normal;
    color: #555555;

}
```

5. Reload `index.html` in your web browser. You should see something similar to the following:

What just happened?

We've just updated the CSS style selector for the default state.

In `index.html`, we created the necessary markup to create a tabs widget. In `index.js`, we have a callback that is executed when the page has finished loading in the web browser. When this happens, our `my_tabs div` turns into a jQuery UI tabs widget. Finally, in `jquery.ui.theme.css`, we've replaced the style selector for the default state. Initially, the theme had three groups in the selector, illustrated as follows:

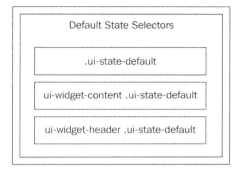

The first selector group selects all elements with the `ui-state-default` class applied to it. The second selector group will select all elements with the `ui-state-default` class applied to it and are nested inside an element with the `ui-widget-content` class applied to it. The last selector, will select all elements with the `ui-state-default` class applied to it and are nested inside an element with the `ui-widget-header` class applied to it.

This group of selectors shares the same style properties. In fact, we didn't actually change any of the style properties for the default state. We simply change the group selector to a simple class selector. We did this by removing the last two groups from the selector. This leaves us with just one class—`ui-state-default`.

This class is what applies the style properties to the elements, not the fact that they're nested inside a `ui-widget-content` or `ui-widget-header` element. The purpose of this example is to highlight that although the default state has fancy group selectors that include the widget container CSS classes, they aren't necessarily required.

Time for action - default link selectors

Similar to the selectors in the previous section, the default state in the jQuery UI CSS framework has selectors that work with links. These styles change the way link elements nested within a default state element look. Additionally, links have pseudo state selectors. Let's see how these are used to effect button widgets:

1. Edit the `index.html` file created earlier and replace the content with the following:

```
<html xmlns="http://www.w3.org/1999/xhtml">

  <head>

    <title>Transforming Interaction States</title>

    <link href="jqueryui/development-
    bundle/themes/base/jquery.ui.all.css" rel="stylesheet"
    type="text/css" />
```

```
            <script src="jqueryui/js/jquery-1.5.x.min.js"
            type="text/javascript"></script>
            <script src="jqueryui/js/jquery-ui-1.8.x.custom.min.js"
            type="text/javascript"></script>
            <script src="index.js" type="text/javascript"></script>

    </head>

    <body style="font-size: 10px;">

        <div class="ui-state-default" style="width: 20%; padding:
        5px;">

                <a href="http://example.com">External Link</a>
                <a href="http://example.org">External Link</a>

        </div>

    </body>

</html>
```

2. Edit the `index.js` file created earlier and replace the content with the following:

```
$(document).ready(function(){

    $("div a").button();

});
```

3. In the `jqueryui/development-bundle/themes/base` directory, edit the `jquery.ui.theme.css` file.

4. Locate the `.ui-state-default a, .ui-state-default a:link, .ui-state-default a:visited` style and replace it with the following:

```
.ui-state-default a, .ui-state-default a:link {

    color: #555555;
    text-decoration: none;

}

.ui-state-default a:visited {

    color: red;

}
```

5. Reload `index.html` in your web browser and click on one of the external links.

6. Once again, reload `index.html` in your web browser. You should see something similar to the following now that one of the links has been visited:

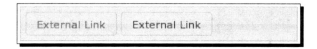

What just happened?

In `index.html`, we've created a simple `div` element and put it in the default state by applying the `ui-state-default` class to it. We've also given the `div` some padding and a width—these are in-line styles and are for illustrative purposes only. Inside the `div`, we have two link elements pointing to two distinct URLs, external to our application.

In `index.js`, we create two button widgets using the two links from `index.html`. We use the `div a` selector as we know that our links are nested in a `div` element.

In `jquery.ui.theme.css`, we've broken style definition for default state links into two styles. We did this by moving the visited pseudo-state for link elements out of the group selector and into its own selector. We then set the color property to red for visited links inside elements with a default state. In the previous screenshot, I clicked on the first External Link and came back to the page. As I've visited this page, the color now shows in red.

The following image illustrates how the color style property is applied to the to button widgets in our example. The `div` that contains the two buttons has all three selectors from the group applied to it:

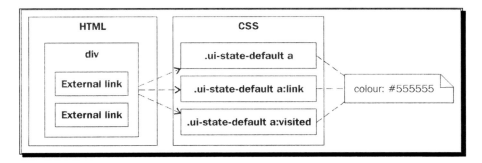

We can see here that elements in the default state will apply the color #555555 to any descendant link elements. The following figure illustrates how the color is applied to our elements after we made the changes to the default state selectors for links:

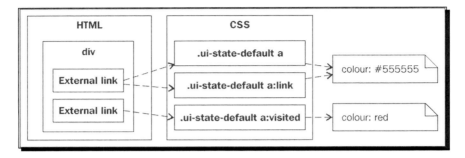

We can see here that button widgets inside an element with the default state have a different color than button widgets that haven't been visited.

Have a go hero

Try removing the .ui-state-default a:link selector from the preceding example. Do unvisited links still look the same, or is this actually required? Try this in several web browsers.

Default state borders

Widgets elements in a default state will inherit border styles. This means that putting something into the default state by applying the ui-state-default class will change the appearance of the borders.

When a page first loads, widget elements that require a border style should have a default state applied to them. This is because there is no other border style inherited from parent theme classes such as ui-widget-content. We use the ui-state-default class to define how the borders of widget elements look before the user has had a chance to interact with them.

Time for action - default border styles

It's time to update the ui-state-default CSS class so we can see how changes to the border style properties affect the appearance of widgets:

1. Edit the index.html file created earlier and replace the content with the following:

   ```
   <html xmlns="http://www.w3.org/1999/xhtml">

       <head>
   ```

```
        <title>Transforming Interaction States</title>

        <link href="jqueryui/development-bundle/themes/base/
        jquery.ui.all.css" rel="stylesheet" type="text/css" />

        <script src="jqueryui/js/jquery-1.5.x.min.js" type="text/
          javascript"></script>
        <script src="jqueryui/js/jquery-ui-1.8.x.custom.min.js"
          type="text/javascript"></script>
        <script src="index.js" type="text/javascript"></script>

    </head>

    <body style="font-size: 10px;">

        <div style="margin-bottom: 5px;">
            <button id="my_button">Click Me</button>
        </div>
        <div>
            <input id="my_datepicker" type="text"/>
        </div>

    </body>

</html>
```

2. Edit the `index.js` file created earlier and replace the content with the following:

```
$(document).ready(function(){

    $("#my_button").button();
    $("#my_datepicker").datepicker();

});
```

3. In the `jqueryui/development-bundle/themes/base` directory, edit the `jquery.ui.theme.css` file.

4. Locate the `.ui-state-default, .ui-widget-content .ui-state-default, .ui-widget-header .ui-state-default` style definition and replace it with the following:

```
.ui-state-default, .ui-widget-content .ui-state-default, .ui-
widget-header .ui-state-default {

    border: 1px dashed red;
```

```
background: #e6e6e6 url(images/ui-bg_glass_75_e6e6e6_1x400.
png) 50% 50% repeat-x;
font-weight: normal;
color: #555555;

}
```

5. Reload `index.html` in your web browser. You should see something similar to the following:

What just happened?

In `index.html`, we have two `div` elements, each of which contains the markup for creating a jQuery UI widget. The `div` is used for a button widget while the second widget is used for a date-picker widget. We've added an in-line style to the first `div` element which provides some space between the two `div` elements. This is only illustrative and not relevant to the example.

In `index.js`, we create a button widget and a date-picker widget using the markup for the two widgets found in `index.html`. These two widget constructors are called when the page has finished loading.

In `jquery.ui.theme.css`, we've updated the border style property for the default state. We've set the border type to dashed and the border color to red. As we can see, the button widget in our example is placed in a default state when the page first loads—this is evident by the red, dashed border. We can also see that the individual day buttons of the date-picker widget have a red, dashed border. However, one of the day buttons doesn't share the same border styles. This element obviously isn't in a default state.

Default state font

As with border styles, the default state changes font style properties when applied to widgets. Widget elements in the default state will inherit font style properties from parent elements. For instance, elements in the default state will inherit the font-family property from the `ui-widget` class.

The `font-family` style property is defined in `ui-widget` so that all widgets in a user interface share the same font type - this probably shouldn't be overridden by any states. However, we might want the `font-weight` and color properties to change based on the state of an element.

Time for action - default font styles

Let's update the `ui-state-default` style definition to use different font properties:

1. Edit the `index.html` file created earlier and replace the content with the following:

```
<html xmlns="http://www.w3.org/1999/xhtml">

    <head>

        <title>Transforming Interaction States</title>

        <link href="jqueryui/development-bundle/themes/base/
          jquery.ui.all.css" rel="stylesheet" type="text/css" />

        <script src="jqueryui/js/jquery-1.5.x.min.js" type="text/
          javascript"></script>
        <script src="jqueryui/js/jquery-ui-1.8.x.custom.min.js"
          type="text/javascript"></script>
        <script src="index.js" type="text/javascript"></script>

    </head>

    <body style="font-size: 10px;">

        <div style="margin-bottom: 5px; width: 40%;">

            <div id="my_tabs">

                <ul>
                    <li><a href="#first">First</a></li>
                    <li><a href="#second">Second</a></li>
                    <li><a href="#third">Third</a></li>
                </ul>

                <div id="first">
                    <p>First paragraph</p>
```

```
                    <p>Second paragraph</p>
                    <p>Third paragraph</p>
                </div>

                <div id="second"></div>
                <div id="third"></div>

            </div>

        </div>

        <div style="margin-bottom: 5px; width: 40%;">

            <div id="my_accordion">

                <h3><a href="#">First</a></h3>
                <div>
                    <p>First paragraph</p>
                    <p>Second paragraph</p>
                    <p>Third paragraph</p>
                </div>

                <h3><a href="#">Second</a></h3>
                <div></div>

                <h3><a href="#">Third</a></h3>
                <div></div>

            </div>

        </div>

        <div>
            <button id="my_button">Click Me</button>
        </div>

    </body>

</html>
```

2. Edit the `index.js` file and replace the content with the following:

```
$(document).ready(function(){

    $("#my_tabs").tabs();
    $("#my_accordion").accordion();
    $("#my_button").button();

});
```

3. In the `jqueryui/development-bundle/themes/base` **directory, edit the** `jquery.ui.theme.css` **file.**

4. Locate the `.ui-state-default, .ui-widget-content .ui-state-default, .ui-widget-header .ui-state-default` style definition and replace it with the following:

```
.ui-state-default, .ui-widget-content .ui-state-default, .ui-
widget-header .ui-state-default {

    border: 1px solid #d3d3d3;
    background: #e6e6e6 url(images/ui-bg_glass_75_e6e6e6_1x400.
    png) 50% 50% repeat-x;
    font-weight: bold;
    color: red;

}
```

5. Reload `index.html` in your web browser. You should see something similar to the following:

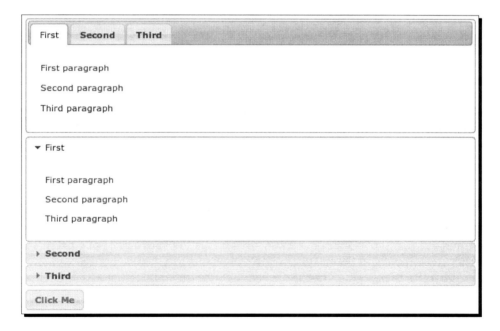

What just happened?

In `index.html`, we have three div elements that accommodate three jQuery UI widgets. We add in-line styles to the first two `div` elements to set the width and to give us some space. These in-line styles are for illustrative purposes only are aren't relevant to what we're trying to show here.

In the first `div`, we created some markup for a tabs widget. In the second `div`, we created markup for an accordion widget. In the last `div`, we created a button element that will serve as the basis for a jQuery UI button widget.

The `index.js` file defines a callback function executed when the page has finished loading in the browser. It is in this function that we're able to build our three widgets—tabs, accordion, and a button.

In `jquery.ui.theme.css`, we've updated the `font-weight` and `color` style properties of the `ui-state-default` class. The `font-weight` for elements in the default state is now bold and the font color is now red. You'll notice that in the tabs an accordion widgets, the font for elements in the default tabs is now bold, but the font color hasn't changed to red. This isn't the case with the button widget - it's font is now bold and red.

This is due to the fact that the font color style properties are overridden for link elements in the default state. But the font-weight isn't and is thus applied here. The text for default tabs and default accordion sections are inside link elements whereas the text for the button element isn't.

Have a go hero

Try modifying the above example to include a `font-style` property for the default state. How does this compare to elements in other states?

Default state background

Just as we can customize the background of widget container CSS classes - `ui-widget-header` and `ui-widget-content`, we can also change the appearance of elements with the default state applied to them. These widget elements use the `ui-state-default` class to define what the background looks like when the user isn't interacting with them in one way or another.

Time for action - default background styles

Changing the background style for the default state is easy. Let's take a closer look at how we can do this:

1. Edit the `index.html` file created earlier and replace the content with the following:

```html
<html xmlns="http://www.w3.org/1999/xhtml">

    <head>

        <title>Transforming Interaction States</title>

        <link href="jqueryui/development-bundle/themes/base/
         jquery.ui.all.css" rel="stylesheet" type="text/css" />

        <script src="jqueryui/js/jquery-1.5.x.min.js" type="text/
         javascript"></script>
        <script src="jqueryui/js/jquery-ui-1.8.x.custom.min.js"
         type="text/javascript"></script>
        <script src="index.js" type="text/javascript"></script>

    </head>

    <body style="font-size: 10px;">

        <div style="margin-bottom: 5px;">

            <button id="my_button">Click Me</button>

        </div>

        <div>

            <input id="my_datepicker" type="text"/>

        </div>

    </body>

</html>
```

2. Edit the `index.js` file created earlier and replace the content with the following:

```javascript
$(document).ready(function(){

    $("#my_button").button();
    $("#my_datepicker").datepicker();

});
```

3. In the `jqueryui/development-bundle/themes/base` directory, edit the `jquery.ui.theme.css` file.

4. Locate the `.ui-state-default, .ui-widget-content .ui-state-default, .ui-widget-header .ui-state-default` style definition and replace it with the following:

```
.ui-state-default, .ui-widget-content .ui-state-default, .ui-
widget-header .ui-state-default {

    border: 1px solid #d3d3d3;
    background-color: #e6e6e6;
    background: -moz-linear-gradient(100% 100% 90deg, #aaaaaa,
    #e6e6e6);
    background: -webkit-gradient(linear, 0% 0%, 0% 100%,
    from(#e6e6e6), to(#aaaaaa));
    font-weight: normal;
    color: #555555;

}
```

5. Reload `index.html` in your web browser. You should see something similar to the following:

What just happened?

In `index.html`, we've created markup for two widgets - a button and a date-picker. The markup for each widget is contained within a `div`.

In `index.js`, we have a callback that is executed when the page loads. This callback creates our button and date-picker widgets.

We've change the `ui-state-default` style definition in `jquery.ui.theme.css`. Here, the background image that gives the default state it's background texture has been removed. We've added two new background properties. First, the `-moz-linear-gradient` defines a CSS3 gradient background for Firefox web browsers. Second, the `-webkit-gradient` defines a CSS3 gradient background for webkit-based browsers (Chrome, Safari).

So you may wonder, why bother removing the background image that works perfectly fine in all browsers? For instance, if you're viewing this page in IE, you wont see a gradient. This is really a conscious decision made by the theme author. By doing this with the background, we're reducing the amount of requests made to the server because no image needs to be retrieved by the browser. On the other hand, our theme is less portable. That is, in browsers that do not support these CSS3 gradient functions, we'll see a flat background color. As always, there are trade-offs to be considered when building software. Thankfully, the jQuery UI theming framework allows us to consider the alternatives.

Pop quiz – the default state

1. Why do widgets need a default state?

   a. jQuery UI widgets always need a state. The default state is active when a widget is first created.

   b. Widgets do not need a default state.

   c. Widgets need a default state because this is how the styles from the theme are applied to them.

2. How is the default state applied to `ui-widget-header` and `ui-widget-content` container elements?

   a. The default state is applied to ui-widget-header and ui-widget-content container elements by using a group selector. This, however, isn't needed. Only the .ui-state-default selector is required.

   b. By using the .ui-state-default selector.

   c. The application developer must manually apply the default state to all widgets.

3. How is the default state applied to links that have been visited?

   a. The default stat is applied to visited links by using the `:visited pseudo` state.

   b. The default state isn't applied to visited links.

   c. The default state is applied to visited links by the `ui-state-default` class alone.

The hover state

When a user first interacts with a widget, it is usually by means of hovering their mouse over it. If the widget, or a component element of the widget, is meant for user interaction, we want to inform the user of this by changing the appearance of the element in a subtle way. I say subtle because hovering over something interactive should give a subtle hint. This might be as simple as change the background opacity or a small change in the font color. Anything more is obtrusive to say the least.

To introduce these changes to widgets when a user hovers over them, we apply the hover state to that element. The `ui-state-hover` CSS class is an essential piece of the jQuery UI theming framework and is the subject of this section.

Hover state selectors

Just as selectors are used to constrain how the default state styles are applied to elements in containers, the hover state uses a similar selector structure. In fact, you'll notice that the selectors are nearly identical aside from the state name.

Another difference, perhaps more obvious, is the length of the selector for the hover state style is twice as long. This is because of the focus state. The `ui-state-focus` class shares the same style definition as that of the `ui-state-hover` class. The reason is simple. Hovering and focusing actions performed by the user represent the same thing. We'll see how this is done in more detail shortly.

Time for action - hover container selectors

It's time to take a look at how the hover state works inside widget containers. To do this, we'll need some sample widgets so let's do that now:

1. Edit the index.html file created earlier, and replace the content with the following:

    ```
    <html xmlns="http://www.w3.org/1999/xhtml">

        <head>

            <title>Transforming Interaction States</title>

            <link href="jqueryui/development-bundle/themes/base/
             jquery.ui.all.css" rel="stylesheet" type="text/css" />

            <script src="jqueryui/js/jquery-1.5.x.min.js" type="text/
             javascript"></script>
            <script src="jqueryui/js/jquery-ui-1.8.x.custom.min.js"
             type="text/javascript"></script>
    ```

```
            <script src="index.js" type="text/javascript"></script>

    </head>

    <body style="font-size: 10px;">

        <div style="width: 40%;">

            <div id="my_tabs">

                <ul>
                    <li><a href="#first">First</a></li>
                    <li><a href="#second">Second</a></li>
                    <li><a href="#third">Third</a></li>
                </ul>

                <div id="first">
                    <p>First paragraph</p>
                    <p>Second paragraph</p>
                    <p>Third paragraph</p>
                </div>

                <div id="second"></div>
                <div id="third"></div>

            </div>

        </div>

    </body>

</html>
```

2. Edit the `index.js` file created earlier and replace the content with the following:

```
$(document).ready(function(){

    $("#my_tabs").tabs();

});
```

3. In the `jqueryui/development-bundle/themes/base` directory, edit the `jquery.ui.theme.css` file.

4. Locate the `.ui-state-hover, .ui-widget-content .ui-state-hover,` `.ui-widget-header .ui-state-hover, .ui-state-focus, .ui-widget-` `content .ui-state-focus, .ui-widget-header .ui-state-focus` style definition and replace it with the following:

```
.ui-state-hover, .ui-widget-content .ui-state-hover, .ui-widget-
header .ui-state-hover, .ui-state-focus, .ui-widget-content .ui-
state-focus, .ui-widget-header .ui-state-focus {

    border: 1px dashed red;
    background: #dadada url(images/ui-bg_glass_75_dadada_1x400.
    png) 50% 50% repeat-x;
    font-weight: normal;
    color: #212121;

}
```

5. Reload index.html in your web browser. You should see something similar to the following:

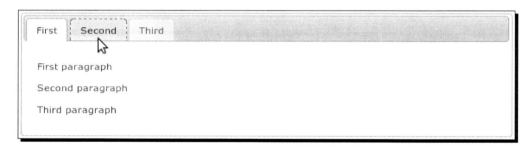

What just happened?

In `index.html`, we've created the markup necessary for a tabs widget. In `index.js`, we call the necessary jQuery UI constructor to create the widget when the page has finished loading. In `jquery.ui.theme.css`, we've changed the border style property for the `ui-state-hover` class to red and dashed.

As we can see, when the user hovers the mouse pointer over one of the tabs, it enters a hover state. This is evidenced by the change in appearance. In our example, the `.ui-widget-header .ui-state-hover` segment of the group would have matched the tab being hovered over. This is because the tab element is within a `ui-widget-header` element.

Hovering and focusing

The ui-state-hover and ui-state-focus CSS classes share the same style definition. There is a good reason for this—hovering and focusing are the essentially the same thing. The only difference is how the user interacts with the widget. The hover state is a little more obvious, the only way a widget element enters a hover state is if the user moves their mouse pointer over the widget in question. By contrast, a widget element enters a focused state when the user either clicks on the element or uses the *Tab* key to change the currently focused widget.

Time for action - separating the hover and focus states

Let's take a look in more detail at the difference between widget elements in hover and focus states:

1. Reuse the content of the index.html and index.js from the previous section. This will create a tabs widget.

2. In the jqueryui/development-bundle/themes/base directory, edit the jquery.ui.theme.css file.

3. Locate the .ui-state-hover, .ui-widget-content .ui-state-hover, .ui-widget-header .ui-state-hover, .ui-state-focus, .ui-widget-content .ui-state-focus, .ui-widget-header .ui-state-focus style definition and replace it with the following:

```
.ui-state-hover, .ui-widget-content .ui-state-hover, .ui-widget-
header .ui-state-hover {

    border: 1px dashed red;
    background: #dadada url(images/ui-bg_glass_75_dadada_1x400.
    png) 50% 50% repeat-x;
    font-weight: normal;
    color: #212121;

}

.ui-state-focus, .ui-widget-content .ui-state-focus, .ui-widget-
header .ui-state-focus {

    border: 1px dashed green;
    background: #dadada url(images/ui-bg_glass_75_dadada_1x400.
    png) 50% 50% repeat-x;
    font-weight: normal;
    color: #212121;

}
```

```
.ui-state-focus a {

    outline: 0;

}
```

4. Reload `index.html` in your web browser. You should see something similar to the following:

What just happened?

We've reused the same tabs widget from the previous example, so nothing has changed with the HTML or JavaScript, in `jquery.ui.theme.css`, we've taken the style definition for the hover state and broken it into three separate definitions. The first is the hover state. We've updated this style to display a red border. The second is the focus state. This style will show a green border around any element is the focus state. The last style definition we've added is new. It affects links nested inside elements in the default state. We've set the outline property to 0. What this does is remove the dotted outline that browsers place around links when they're focused. We only want border styles from our theme, not what the browser thinks it should look like.

In this example, you can see I've tabbed my way over to the second tab which puts it in a focused state. I'm also hovering over the third tab which puts it in a hover state. Before we made the changes to the theme, these two tabs would have looked identical. But we've separated the two state styles and thus get a different look.

Have a go hero

Try separating the preceding example further. For instance, maybe you want to the hover state to look different for `ui-widget-header` and `ui-widget-content` elements.

Hover state font

As with the default state, we have the ability to define font style properties for elements in the hover state. For instance, we may want to change the boldness or the color of the element font when the user moves the mouse pointer over it.

We can use the ThemeRoller application to define the border, and background styles of the hover state class. We can also use the ThemeRoller to color of the font for hover states. However, we'll have to manipulate the theme CSS directly to change other font properties. For example, if we want text in a hover state bold, we can't do this with the ThemeRoller.

Time for action - hover font styles

Here, we're going to update the `ui-state-hover` class to change the appearance of the font when a user hovers over widget components:

1. Edit the `index.html` file created earlier and replace the content with the following:

```html
<html xmlns="http://www.w3.org/1999/xhtml">

    <head>

        <title>Transforming Interaction States</title>

        <link href="jqueryui/development-
        bundle/themes/base/jquery.ui.all.css" rel="stylesheet"
        type="text/css" />

        <script src="jqueryui/js/jquery-1.5.x.min.js"
        type="text/javascript"></script>
        <script src="jqueryui/js/jquery-ui-1.8.x.custom.min.js"
        type="text/javascript"></script>
        <script src="index.js" type="text/javascript"></script>

    </head>

    <body style="font-size: 10px;">

        <div style="width: 40%;">

            <div id="my_accordion">

                <h3><a href="#">First</a></h3>
                <div>
                    <p>First paragraph</p>
                    <p>Second paragraph</p>
                    <p>Third paragraph</p>
                </div>

                <h3><a href="#">Second</a></h3>
                <div></div>

                <h3><a href="#">Third</a></h3>
                <div></div>
```

```
                    </div>

                </div>

            </body>

        </html>
```

2. Edit the `index.js` file created earlier and replace the content with the following:

```
$(document).ready(function(){

    $("#my_accordion").accordion();

});
```

3. In the `jqueryui/development-bundle/themes/base` directory, edit the `jquery.ui.theme.css` file.

4. Locate the `.ui-state-hover, .ui-widget-content .ui-state-hover, .ui-widget-header .ui-state-hover, .ui-state-focus, .ui-widget-content .ui-state-focus, .ui-widget-header .ui-state-focus` style definition and replace it with the following:

```
.ui-state-hover, .ui-widget-content .ui-state-hover, .ui-widget-
header .ui-state-hover, .ui-state-focus, .ui-widget-content .ui-
state-focus, .ui-widget-header .ui-state-focus {

    border: 1px solid #999999;
    background: #dadada url(images/ui-bg_glass_75_dadada_1x400.
png) 50% 50% repeat-x;
    font-weight: bold;
    color: #666666;

}
```

5. Reload `index.html` in your web browser. You should see something similar to the following:

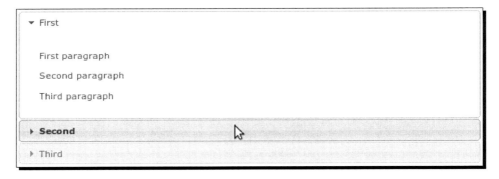

What just happened?

In `index.html`, we've created the markup for a basic accordion widget. The index.js file creates the jQuery UI component when the page has finished loading.

In `jquery.ui.theme.css`, we've altered the color property of the `ui-state-hover` and `ui-state-focus` classes. We've also set the `font-weight` property to bold for both of these classes. This we cannot do with the ThemeRoller application as there is no separation of font properties between states when building themes this way.

You can see in the example that when I move my mouse pointer over the second accordion segment, the font properties change.

Pop quiz – the hover state

1. What is the difference between the hover state and the focus state?

    a. The hover state is used to indicate the user has moved their mouse pointer over something actionable. The focus state is used to indicate which widget component is ready for action. Visually, there is no difference between the two states.

    b. The focus state can only by applied when the user interacts with the page using their keyboard while the hover state can only be applied using the mouse pointer.

    c. The hover state looks different visually from the hover state.

2. How do you separate the hover state and focus state style definitions?

    a. The hover and focus states can be separated and modified independently of one another by breaking the group CSS selector for the two classes into their own selectors.

    b. The two states cannot be separated.

    c. The two states can only be separated by modifying the jQuery UI widget code.

3. How does the hover state get applied to widget components?

    a. Each jQuery UI widget is responsible for applying the ui-state-hover class to its components by listening for mouse events.)

    b. The hover state is applied by using the `:hover pseudo` CSS class.

    c. The hover state must be manually applied to application developers using jQuery UI widgets.

The active state

So far, we've seen the default state, what a widget looks like before the user starts interacting with it, and the hover state, what a widget looks like when a user moves the mouse pointer over a widget component. The focus state is essentially the same thing as the hover state—it is applied differently.

What defines how widgets look when the user actually clicks something? In some cases, when a widget is clicked, part of that widget becomes active. For instance, the user selects a tab or expands an accordion segment. When this happens, the selected element should look different than the other, inactive widget elements. With the jQuery UI theming framework, we apply the `ui-state-active` class to these elements.

Active state selectors

The CSS selectors that determine how the style properties of the `ui-state-active` class are applied to widget elements are no different from those of the default and hover states. The active state uses widget containers as part of its select- `ui-widget-content` and `ui-widget-header`.

Time for action - active container selectors

It's time to take a closer look at how the CSS selectors that apply the active state style properties are applied to jQuery UI elements.

1. Edit the `index.html` file created earlier and replace the content with the following:

```
<html xmlns="http://www.w3.org/1999/xhtml">

    <head>

        <title>Transforming Interaction States</title>

        <link href="jqueryui/development-bundle/themes/base/
        jquery.ui.all.css" rel="stylesheet" type="text/css" />

        <script src="jqueryui/js/jquery-1.5.x.min.js" type="text/
        javascript"></script>
        <script src="jqueryui/js/jquery-ui-1.8.x.custom.min.js"
        type="text/javascript"></script>
        <script src="index.js" type="text/javascript"></script>

    </head>

    <body style="font-size: 10px;">

        <div style="width: 40%;">
```

```
<div id="my_tabs">

    <ul>
        <li><a href="#first">First</a></li>
        <li><a href="#second">Second</a></li>
        <li><a href="#third">Third</a></li>
    </ul>

    <div id="first">
        <p>First paragraph</p>
        <p>Second paragraph</p>
        <p>Third paragraph</p>
    </div>

    <div id="second"></div>
    <div id="third"></div>

</div>

</body>

</html>
```

2. Edit the `index.js` file created earlier and replace the content with the following:

```
$(document).ready(function(){

    $("#my_tabs").tabs();

});
```

3. In the `jqueryui/development-bundle/themes/base` directory, edit the `jquery.ui.theme.css` file.

4. Locate the `.ui-state-active, .ui-widget-content .ui-state-active, .ui-widget-header .ui-state-active` style definition and replace it with the following:

```
.ui-state-active, .ui-widget-content .ui-state-active, .ui-widget-
header .ui-state-active {

    border: 1px dashed red;
    background: #ffffff url(images/ui-bg_glass_65_ffffff_1x400.
png) 50% 50% repeat-x;
    font-weight: normal;
    color: #212121;

}
```

5. Reload `index.html` in your web browser. You should see something similar to the following:

What just happened?

As with several previous examples in this chapter, we've created a simple tabs widget by defining the necessary markup in `index.html` and instantiating the widget in `index.js`.

To help us see where the selectors for the active state are applied, we've updated the border style property to use a dashed, red border. As we can see, when we first load the page, the first tabs is selected by default. The border style change we made is applied by the `.ui-widget-header .ui-state-active` part of the group selector that applies the styles of the active state.

We can also see that the bottom part of the border surrounding the selected tab doesn't reflect the changes we've just made. This is a good example of how styles specific to the widget can override those of the theme. In this case, specific styles for the tabs widget override those of the active state in the theme.

Have a go hero

The preceding example used a dashed, red border to illustrate where the change in the widget was made. Modify it to use styles that look like they're part of the theme.

Active state background

Widgets enter an active state when the user starts using it. For instance, by selecting the component. The user needs to be able to differentiate between what is active inside a widget and what isn't. A good visual pointer to something that is active is the background color. We have the ability in the jQuery UI theming framework to adjust the active state background styles to our liking.

Time for action - active background styles

It's time to customize the background styles of our theme for widget elements that have entered an active state:

1. Edit the `index.html` file created earlier and replace the content with the following:

```
<html xmlns="http://www.w3.org/1999/xhtml">

    <head>

        <title>Transforming Interaction States</title>

        <link href="jqueryui/development-bundle/themes/base/
          jquery.ui.all.css" rel="stylesheet" type="text/css" />

        <script src="jqueryui/js/jquery-1.5.x.min.js" type="text/
          javascript"></script>
        <script src="jqueryui/js/jquery-ui-1.8.x.custom.min.js"
          type="text/javascript"></script>
        <script src="index.js" type="text/javascript"></script>

    </head>

    <body style="font-size: 10px;">

        <div id="my_buttonset">
            <input type="radio" id="first" name="radio" />
            <label for="first">First</label>
            <input type="radio" id="second" name="radio" />
            <label for="second">Second</label>
            <input type="radio" id="third" name="radio" />
            <label for="third">Third</label>
        </div>

    </body>

</html>
```

2. Edit the `index.js` file created earlier and replace the content with the following:

```
$(document).ready(function(){

    $("#my_buttonset").buttonset();

});
```

3. In the `jqueryui/development-bundle/themes/base` directory, edit the `jquery.ui.theme.css` file.

4. Locate the `.ui-state-active, .ui-widget-content .ui-state-active, .ui-widget-header .ui-state-active` style definition and replace it with the following:

```
.ui-state-active, .ui-widget-content .ui-state-active, .ui-widget-
header .ui-state-active {

    border: 1px solid #aaaaaa;
    background: #ffffff;
    font-weight: normal;
    color: #212121;

}
```

5. Reload `index.html` in your web browser. You should see something similar to the following:

What just happened?

We've created a button-set widget, a group of buttons in which only one is selected at any given time. In `index.html`, we use a set of radio button elements as the basis for building the button-set widget. In `index.js`, we created the widget using the markup from `index.html`.

In `jquery.ui.theme.css`, we've updated the background style in the `ui-state-active` class. We removed the background image from the active state. This didn't have any impact on the appearance of the button-set widget as we can see from the output - it looks the same as it did before we altered the theme.

As we can see, this change highlights the fact that theme authors also need to consider the less-tangible changes made to themes. We decided that the theme we're building will use a solid color for the background of the active state instead of including an image overlay. This doesn't have an obvious impact as far as the end user is concerned, but it does simplify the theme code.

Summary

We've learned a lot in this chapter about widget states and how they're applied to widgets. Not all jQuery UI widgets have states but only those the user interacts with. It is this user interaction that causes widgets to change state.

All styles that visually reflect a change in state to the user are defined in CSS classes in the theming framework. By default, there are three distinct states within the framework—default, hover, and active. There is a fourth state, focus, which is essentially the same thing as the hover state.

Interaction states are meant to indicate to the user that they're on the right path. For instance, if a user hovers over something that may be clicked such as a button, the button should change slightly.

Once the user has finished interacting with the user interface, they need feedback to indicate that something happened. This is the topic of the next chapter.

6

Customizing Interaction Cues

In the previous chapter, we explored interaction states—visual indicators for the end user. Interaction cues are similar to states in that they're visual indicators, marking some event that has taken place. Cues are a little more subtle than states – they often guide the user to their next course of action.

In this chapter, we shall:

◆ See the difference between states and cues

◆ Display information cues

◆ Display errors

◆ Work with priorities

So let's get on with it.

What are interaction cues?

In the previous chapter, we saw how interaction states help guide the user in their course of action. We apply CSS classes from the jQuery UI theming framework to show a change in state. These changes in state are triggered by the user's actions.

Interaction cues are similar to interaction states, the key difference being that they are generated by the application, not necessarily the user hovering over a button, say. The user needs to be informed of important events in the application, such as a record being created or an error in retrieving a list of products. Without this feedback, the user begins to feel lost.

In addition to cuing raw information about events taking place in the system, we can also use interaction cues to guide the user. For instance, we might want to indicate that a certain widget is disabled due to lack of permissions. This doesn't warrant a message being displayed since they can still use other page elements. Another example of information cues displayed to the user is something taking the priority over another element. For example, correcting errors when filling out a form.

We'll spend the duration of this chapter going into more detail about each interaction cue and how they can be used to effectively grab the user's attention.

Time for action - preparing the example

It's time to set up an environment for examples throughout the remainder of this chapter. As mentioned in the previous chapter, it is best that you restore the state of your example environment using the steps here. This only applies if you've been following examples from the previous chapters:

1. If you haven't already, download and extract the jQuery UI package into a directory called `jqueryui` from `http://jqueryui.com/download`.

2. At the same level as the `jqueryui` directory, create a new `index.html` file with the following content:

```
<html xmlns="http://www.w3.org/1999/xhtml">

    <head>

        <title>Customizing Interaction Cues</title>

        <link href="jqueryui/development-
        bundle/themes/base/jquery.ui.all.css" rel="stylesheet"
        type="text/css" />

        <script src="jqueryui/js/jquery-1.5.x.min.js"
        type="text/javascript"></script>
        <script src="jqueryui/js/jquery-ui-1.8.x.custom.min.js"""
        type="text/javascript"></script>
        <script src="index.js" type="text/javascript"></script>

    </head>

    <body style="font-size: 10px;">

        <button id="my_button">Click Me</button>

    </body>

</html>
```

3. At the same level as the `jqueryui` directory, create a new `index.js` file with the following content:

```
$(document).ready(function(){

    $("#my_button").button();

});
```

4. Open `index.html` in your web browser; you should see something similar to the following:

What just happened?

As with the previous chapters, we've set up an environment we can use as the basis for our examples throughout the chapter.

In `index.html`, we include the necessary jQuery UI theme stylesheet, the core jQuery library, as well as the jQuery UI widget library. We've also created a button element to use as the basis for the button widget.

In `index.js`, we actually create the jQuery UI button widget when the page has finished loading. If you see the button widget as illustrated above, your example environment is ready to go. Let's proceed with developing some interaction cue theme designs.

The highlight state

Sometimes we want to show our web application user an informative message. These are brief messages, usually no longer than a line or two, that tell the user something has happened. We saw in the previous chapter that we can use interaction states to inform the user on how to interact with widgets in our user interface. Displaying a message is a more explicit way to communicate feedback.

An appropriate time to display informative messages is when something has changed in the state of the application. For instance, a user might update their user profile data. They have no way of knowing whether the update was successful unless the user interface tells them. Here, application data has changed. We therefore want to explicitly say what has happened using "Profile successfully updated". It is hard to convey this event without text.

The highlight state allows us to combine visual and textual cues into informative messages. The highlight state is part of the jQuery UI theming framework and can be modified to fit our application's style requirements. We'll now take a closer look at what we can do with the highlight interaction cue.

Highlight borders

When we display a message to a user, intended to highlight some event, we're surrounding the text with the highlight state. Like the `ui-widget-content` class, the `ui-state-highlight` class defines borders. The borders can make the message stand out, which is ideal as we want to call attention to it. The border styles of the `ui-state-highlight` class may not fit with the rest of your application's look and feel. We can address this by manipulating the CSS responsible for highlighted message borders.

Time for action - highlight message borders

It's time to create a basic informational message and experiment with the border styles by changing properties in the `ui-state-highlight` class:

1. Edit the index.html file created earlier and replace the content with the following:

    ```
    <html xmlns="http://www.w3.org/1999/xhtml">

        <head>

            <title>Customizing Interaction Cues</title>

            <link href="jqueryui/development-bundle/themes/base/
             jquery.ui.all.css" rel="stylesheet" type="text/css" />

            <script src="jqueryui/js/jquery-1.5.x.min.js" type="text/
             javascript"></script>
            <script src="jqueryui/js/jquery-ui-1.8.x.custom.min.js"
             type="text/javascript"></script>
            <script src="index.js" type="text/javascript"></script>

        </head>

        <body style="font-size: 10px;">

                <div class="ui-widget">

                        <div class="ui-state-highlight ui-corner-all"
                         style="margin-top: 20px; padding: 0 5px;
                         width: 30%;">
                                <p>
                        <span class="ui-icon ui-icon-info"
                         style="float: left; margin-right: .3px;">
                         </span>
    ```

```
                    User profile successfully updated.
          </p>
                </div>

          </div>

      </body>

  </html>
```

2. In the `jqueryui/development-bundle/themes/base` directory, edit the `jquery.ui.theme.css` file.

3. Locate the `.ui-state-highlight, .ui-widget-content .ui-state-highlight, .ui-widget-header .ui-state-highlight` style definition and replace it with the following:

```
.ui-state-highlight, .ui-widget-content .ui-state-highlight, .ui-widget-header .ui-state-highlight  {

    border: 2px solid #fcefa1;
    background: #fbf9ee url(images/ui-bg_glass_55_fbf9ee_1x400.
    png) 50% 50% repeat-x;
    color: #363636;

}
```

4. Reload `index.html` in your web browser. You should see something similar to the following:

> ⓘ User profile successfully updated.

What just happened?

We've just created a highlighted message and displayed it to the user. In `index.html`, our message is made up of two `div` elements, one nested inside the other. The outer `div` is a container for the message. It uses the `ui-widget` CSS class to apply the font settings from our theme. The inner `div` is where we apply the `ui-state-highlight` class, which gives the message it's character. We've also given the message rounded corners by applying the `ui-corner-all` class. We'll learn more about this in a later chapter. There are also some inline styles applied to the inner `div` that are only for layout purposes and aren't relevant to the highlighted state.

Inside the inner `div`, we've added an "information" icon. This further emphasizes to the user that we're displaying a message. The icon we used here is also part of the jQuery UI theming framework and will be covered in more detail in a later chapter. Finally, we have the text that makes up the content of our message.

In `jquery.ui.theme.css`, we've updated the `border` style property in the `ui-state-highlight` class. We've changed the border width from `1px` to `2px`. This gives our informational message even more emphasis.

Time for action - highlight button borders

It's time to see our theme changes from the previous example applied to a button widget:

1. Edit the `index.html` file created earlier and replace the content with the following:

```html
<html xmlns="http://www.w3.org/1999/xhtml">

    <head>

        <title>Customizing Interaction Cues</title>

        <link href="jqueryui/development-bundle/themes/base/
         jquery.ui.all.css" rel="stylesheet" type="text/css" />

        <script src="jqueryui/js/jquery-1.5.x.min.js"
        type="text/javascript"></script>
        <script src="jqueryui/js/jquery-ui-1.8.x.custom.min.js"
        type="text/javascript"></script>
        <script src="index.js" type="text/javascript"></script>

    </head>

    <body style="font-size: 10px;">

        <button id="my_first_button">Normal Button</button>
        <button id="my_second_button">Highlighted Button</button>

    </body>

</html>
```

2. Edit the `index.js` file created earlier and replace the content with the following:

```javascript
$(document).ready(function(){

    $("#my_first_button").button();
    $("#my_second_button").button().addClass("ui-state-
    highlight");

});
```

3. Reuse the changes made to `jquery.ui.theme.css` in the previous example. This will preserve the changes made to the border style property of the `ui-stat-highlight` class.

4. Reload `index.html` in your web browser. You should see something similar to the following:

What just happened?

In `index.html`, we've created the markup necessary for two button widgets using two `button` elements.

In `index.js`, we create two jQuery UI button widgets in the callback function executed when the page has finished loading. The first button is created as a normal button widget. The second button, once created, has the `ui-state-highlight` CSS class applied to it by means of the `addClass()` function.

We can see the difference in appearance between the two buttons—the highlighted button stands out relative to the normal button. We can also see our border changes made in the previous example applied here to the button widget as well.

Highlight background

We can use the `ui-state-highlight` class to apply specific background styles to elements that need emphasis. There are controls in the ThemeRoller application that allow us to customize the highlight state background properties. We can also directly manipulate the style sheet as we'll see next.

Time for action - highlight message background

It's time to change the `background` style properties of the highlight state:

1. In the `index.html` file created earlier, replace the content with the following:

```
<html xmlns="http://www.w3.org/1999/xhtml">

    <head>

        <title>Customizing Interaction Cues</title>

        <link href="jqueryui/development-
        bundle/themes/base/jquery.ui.all.css" rel="stylesheet"
        type="text/css" />
```

```html
            <script src="jqueryui/js/jquery-1.5.x.min.js"
            type="text/javascript"></script>
            <script src="jqueryui/js/jquery-ui-1.8.x.custom.min.js"
            type="text/javascript"></script>
            <script src="index.js" type="text/javascript"></script>

    </head>

  <body style="font-size: 10px;">

    <div class="ui-widget">

      <div class="ui-state-highlight ui-corner-all"
        style="margin-top: 20px; padding: 0 5px; width: 30%;">
        <p>
          <span class="ui-icon ui-icon-info"
          style="float: left; margin-right: 3px;"></span>
            User profile successfully updated.
        </p>
      </div>

    </div>

  </body>

</html>
```

2. In the `jqueryui/development-bundle/themes/base` directory, edit the `jquery.ui.theme.css` file.

3. Locate the `.ui-state-highlight, .ui-widget-content .ui-state-highlight, .ui-widget-header .ui-state-highlight` style definition and replace it with the following:

```css
.ui-state-highlight, .ui-widget-content .ui-state-highlight, .ui-
widget-header .ui-state-highlight  {

    border: 1px solid #fcefa1;
    background: #fbf9ee;
    color: #363636;

}
```

4. Reload `index.html` in your web browser; you should see something similar to the following:

ⓘ User profile successfully updated.

What just happened?

In `index.html`, we've created an informational message to display for the user. This isn't a jQuery UI widget - it consists of regular HTML elements with CSS classes from the jQuery UI theming framework applied to them.

In `jquery.ui.theme.css`, we've updated the `background` style property of the `ui-state-highlight` class. The changes aren't visually striking; all we've done is remove the background image that gave things in a highlighted state their texture. In our example, the simple display message uses a solid color for the background and as a result, doesn't need to download an image from the server.

Time for action - highlight date-picker background

It's time to see our theme changes from the previous example applied to a date-picker widget:

1. Edit the `index.html` file created earlier and replace the content with the following:

```
<html xmlns="http://www.w3.org/1999/xhtml">

    <head>

        <title>Customizing Interaction Cues</title>

        <link href="jqueryui/development-bundle/themes/base/
        jquery.ui.all.css" rel="stylesheet" type="text/css" />

        <script src="jqueryui/js/jquery-1.5.x.min.js" type="text/
        javascript"></script>
        <script src="jqueryui/js/jquery-ui-1.8.x.custom.min.js"
        type="text/javascript"></script>
        <script src="index.js" type="text/javascript"></script>

    </head>

    <body style="font-size: 10px;">

        <input id="my_datepicker" type="text"/>

    </body>

</html>
```

2. Edit the `index.js` file created earlier and replace the content with the following:

```
$(document).ready(function(){

    $('#my_datepicker').datepicker();

});
```

3. Reuse the changes made to `jquery.ui.theme.css` in the previous example. This will preserve the changes made to the `background` property of the `ui-state-highlight` class.

4. Reload `index.html` in your web browser. You should see something similar to the following:

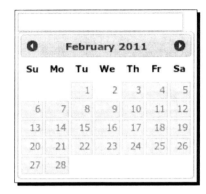

What just happened?

We just made a style update to the date-picker widget with our latest theme update. The current day in the date-picker widget has the `ui-state-highlight` class applied to it.

In `index.html`, we have a simple `input` element that serves as the basis of the date-picker widget. In `index.js`, we create the date-picker widget from the jQuery UI library. We haven't changed anything in `jquery.ui.theme.css` from the previous example.

This is an example of how we can use the highlight state to bring the user's attention to a particular part of a widget; in this case, it is the current date.

Highlight font

When displaying an informational message to a user, or changing the look of an existing widget component by applying the `ui-state-highlight` class, we have the option to change the font styles. This means the color, the font family, or anything we feel better suits highlighted elements in our theme.

Time for action - highlight message font

It's time to change the font style properties of the `ui-state-highlight` class and see how they look when applied to an informational message displayed to the user:

1. Edit the `index.html` file created earlier and replace the content with the following:

```html
<html xmlns="http://www.w3.org/1999/xhtml">

    <head>

        <title>Customizing Interaction Cues</title>

        <link href="jqueryui/development-bundle/themes/base/
jquery.ui.all.css" rel="stylesheet" type="text/css" />

        <script src="jqueryui/js/jquery-1.5.x.min.js" type="text/
javascript"></script>
        <script src="jqueryui/js/jquery-ui-1.8.x.custom.min.js"
type="text/javascript"></script>
        <script src="index.js" type="text/javascript"></script>

    </head>

    <body style="font-size: 10px;">

            <div class="ui-widget">

                    <div class="ui-state-highlight ui-corner-all"
style="margin-top: 20px; padding: 0 5px; width: 30%;">
                            <p>
                    <span class="ui-icon ui-icon-info"
style="float: left; margin-right: .3px;"></span>
                    User profile successfully updated.
            </p>
                    </div>

            </div>

    </body>

</html>
```

2. In the `jqueryui/development-bundle/themes/base` directory, edit the `jquery.ui.theme.css` file.

3. Locate the `.ui-state-highlight, .ui-widget-content .ui-state-highlight, .ui-widget-header .ui-state-highlight` style definition and replace it with the following:

```
.ui-state-highlight, .ui-widget-content .ui-state-highlight, .ui-widget-header .ui-state-highlight {

    border: 1px solid #fcefa1;
    background: #fbf9ee url(images/ui-bg_glass_55_fbf9ee_1x400.
png) 50% 50% repeat-x;
    color: #030303;
    font-weight: bold;

}
```

4. Reload `index.html` in your web browser. You should see something similar to the following:

> ⓘ **User profile successfully updated.**

What just happened?

As with the previous examples where we're displaying an informative message to the user, we've done the same in the `index.html` file here.

In jquery.ui.theme.css, we updated the font `color` and the `font-weight` style properties of the `ui-state-highlight` class. The font color of the message displayed to the user is now darker and the font weight is now bolder.

Time for action - highlight tabs font

Let's reuse the style changes we've just made to our theme and apply the `ui-state-highlight` class to a tabs widget and see how they look:

1. Edit the `index.html` file created earlier and replace the content with the following:

```
<html xmlns="http://www.w3.org/1999/xhtml">

    <head>

        <title>Customizing Interaction Cues</title>

        <link href="jqueryui/development-bundle/themes/base/
          jquery.ui.all.css" rel="stylesheet" type="text/css" />
```

```html
<script src="jqueryui/js/jquery-1.5.x.min.js" type="text/
   javascript"></script>
<script src="jqueryui/js/jquery-ui-1.8.x.custom.min.js"
   type="text/javascript"></script>
<script src="index.js" type="text/javascript"></script>

</head>

<body style="font-size: 10px;">

   <div style="margin-bottom: 5px; width: 40%;">

      <div id="my_tabs">

         <ul>
            <li><a href="#first">First</a></li>
            <li><a href="#second">Second</a></li>
            <li><a href="#third">Third</a></li>
         </ul>

         <div id="first">
            <p>First paragraph</p>
            <p>Second paragraph</p>
            <p>Third paragraph</p>
         </div>

         <div id="second"></div>
         <div id="third"></div>

      </div>

   </div>

</body>

</html>
```

2. Edit the `index.js` file created earlier and replace the content with the following:

```js
$(document).ready(function(){

   $("#my_tabs").tabs();
   $("a[href='#third']").parent().addClass("ui-state-highlight");

});
```

3. Reuse the changes made to the `jquery.ui.theme.css` file in the previous example. This will preserve the changes made to the `color` and `font-weight` properties of the `ui-state-highlight` class.

4. Reload `index.html` in your web browser. You should see something similar to the following:

What just happened?

We've applied the changes we made to the `ui-state-highlight` class in the previous example to the tabs widget.

In `index.html`, we've created the markup necessary to construct a sample jQuery UI tabs widget.

In `index.js`, we have a callback function that is executed when the page has finished loading. This function creates the tab widget. Once the tabs widget is built, we apply the `ui-state-highlight` class to the third tab. We do this by selecting the "a" element with the appropriate `href` attribute; in this case, `#third`. Next, we retrieve the parent element, a `li` element, so we can apply the highlight class.

In this example, we might want to draw the user's attention to the third tab after something they've done in the first tab. Perhaps this changed the state of an application entity currently displayed in the third tab. Or maybe something was being processed in the background and has completed, the result of which is reflected in the third tab. We want to point this completion out to the user.

You'll also notice that the tabs widget has no native way to indicate that a tab should be highlighted. We've imposed a new class on the third tab in our example - the tabs widget isn't expecting a tab to be in a highlighted state. However, this example shows us the power and flexibility of the jQuery UI theming framework. With very little effort and even less hacking, we're able to make the widget look how we want it to while remaining in the confines of the theme structure.

Pop quiz – the highlight state

1. When does it make sense to apply the highlight state?

    a. You apply the highlight state when you need to draw the user's attention to something that just happened. For instance, a notification message.

    b. It only makes sense to apply the highlight state to buttons once they've been clicked.

    c. The highlight state can only be applied to jQuery UI widgets once they've been created.

2. Does the highlight state affect theme icons?

    a. The highlight state changes the icon color.

    b. The highlight state will only affect icons that support it.

    c. The highlight state has no effect when applied to icons.

3. Do any jQuery UI widgets automatically apply the highlight state?

    a. The date-picker widget automatically applies the highlight state to the selected day

    b. Most widgets will accept a parameter that will enable the highlight state when created.

    c. No widgets will automatically apply the highlight state.

The error state

In addition to displaying informative messages to the user, messages that indicate something has happened, we also need to display errors as they take place. Errors also describe something that has taken place, an event in the application. These messages are different though—they're exceptional occurrences that fall outside of the normal workflow. Therefore, we might want to give error messages a distinct look, one that cues the user's attention that something went wrong.

The jQuery UI theming framework provides us with an error state for this purpose. Using the `ui-state-error` class, we can alter the appearance of messages and widget components in such a way that the user sees that something is wrong. Just as we've seen with the highlight state, we're free to customize the error state for our theme as we please.

Error borders

HTML elements stand out more when they have borders with well-defined styles—the color, the thickness. This is especially important when putting something on a web page into an error state. The border styles defined in the `ui-state-error` class should help exemplify that an erroneous event has taken place.

Time for action - error message borders

It's time to modify the border styles of the `ui-state-error` class. We have the option of using the ThemeRoller application to alter the error state border styles, but here, we're going to take a closer look at the underlying CSS:

1. Edit the `index.html` file created earlier and replace the content with the following:

```
<html xmlns="http://www.w3.org/1999/xhtml">

    <head>

        <title>Customizing Interaction Cues</title>

        <link href="jqueryui/development-bundle/themes/base/
jquery.ui.all.css" rel="stylesheet" type="text/css" />

        <script src="jqueryui/js/jquery-1.5.x.min.js" type="text/
javascript"></script>
        <script src="jqueryui/js/jquery-ui-1.8.x.custom.min.js"
type="text/javascript"></script>
        <script src="index.js" type="text/javascript"></script>

    </head>

    <body style="font-size: 10px;">

            <div class="ui-widget">

                    <div class="ui-state-error ui-corner-all"
style="margin-top: 20px; padding: 0 5px; width: 30%;">
                        <p>
                        <span class="ui-icon ui-icon-alert"
style="float: left; margin-right: .3px;"></span>
                        User profile update failed.
                </p>
                    </div>

                </div>

        </body>

    </html>
```

2. In the `jqueryui/development-bundle/themes/base` directory, edit the `jquery.ui.theme.css` file.

3. Locate the `.ui-state-error, .ui-widget-content .ui-state-error, .ui-widget-header .ui-state-error` style definition and replace it with the following:

```
.ui-state-error, .ui-widget-content .ui-state-error, .ui-widget-
header .ui-state-error {

    border: 2px solid #cd0a0a;
    background: #fef1ec url(images/ui-bg_glass_95_fef1ec_1x400.
png) 50% 50% repeat-x;
    color: #cd0a0a;

}
```

4. Reload `index.html` in your web browser. You should see something similar to the following:

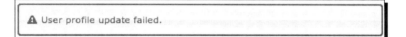

What just happened?

In `index.html`, we've displayed an error message to the user. The HTML elements used to create the message follow the same basic structure as those used to create the informational message earlier in the chapter. The difference is that the inner div element has the `ui-state-error` class applied to it and the `span` element responsible for the icon element has the `ui-icon-alert` class.

In `jquery.ui.theme.css`, we've changed the `border` thickness from 1px to 2px. The remainder of the `ui-state-error` style properties remain unchanged. We can see the thicker red border around our error message, which really makes it stand out.

Time for action - error tabs border

Let's reuse our style updates from the previous example and apply the theme changes to a tabs widget:

1. Edit the `index.html` file created earlier and replace the content with the following:

```
<html xmlns="http://www.w3.org/1999/xhtml">

    <head>
```

```
            <title>Customizing Interation Cues</title>

            <link href="jqueryui/development-bundle/themes/base/
jquery.ui.all.css" rel="stylesheet" type="text/css" />

            <script src="jqueryui/js/jquery-1.5.x.min.js" type="text/
javascript"></script>
            <script src="jqueryui/js/jquery-ui-1.8.x.custom.min.js"
type="text/javascript"></script>
            <script src="index.js" type="text/javascript"></script>

      </head>

      <body style="font-size: 10px;">

            <div style="margin-bottom: 5px; width: 40%;">

                  <div id="my_tabs">

                        <ul>
                              <li><a href="#first">First</a></li>
                              <li><a href="#second">Second</a></li>
                              <li><a href="#third">Third</a></li>
                        </ul>

                        <div id="first">
                              <p>First paragraph</p>
                              <p>Second paragraph</p>
                              <p>Third paragraph</p>
                        </div>

                        <div id="second"></div>
                        <div id="third"></div>

                  </div>

            </div>

      </body>

</html>
```

2. Edit the `index.js` file created earlier and replace the content with the following:

```
$(document).ready(function(){

    $("#my_tabs").tabs();
    $("a[href='#third']").parent().addClass("ui-state-error");

});
```

3. Reuse the changes made to the `jquery.ui.theme.css` file in the previous example. This will preserve the changes made to the `border` property of the `ui-state-error` class.

4. Reload `index.html` in your web browser. You should see something similar to the following:

What just happened?

We've applied the changes we made in the previous example, setting the border thickness in the `ui-state-error` class, to a tabs widget.

In `index.html`, we created the necessary markup to build a jQuery UI tabs widget. In `index.js`, we construct the tabs widget once the page load has completed. Once the tabs widget has been built, we then apply the error state to the third tab.

What this example shows is that something went wrong in the third tab. As there is a very good chance that some asynchronous HTTP requests are being made in our hypothetical application, there is also a good chance that the user moves on to another task before the server responds. So in our example, the user might have done something in the third tab that initiated an HTTP request and gone back to the first tab. The server then responds with an error. Rather than stating "by the way, you have an error tab"," we give the user a much more effective visual cue. This is easy with the error state as we've just seen—one line of code to apply it.

Error background

Like the highlight state background, theme authors can also customize the background of the error state.

Time for action - error message background

Let's update the background styles of the `ui-state-error` class:

1. Edit the `index.html` file created earlier and replace the content with the following:

```
<html xmlns="http://www.w3.org/1999/xhtml">

    <head>

        <title>Customizing Interaction Cues</title>

        <link href="jqueryui/development-bundle/themes/base/
jquery.ui.all.css" rel="stylesheet" type="text/css" />

        <script src="jqueryui/js/jquery-1.5.x.min.js" type="text/
javascript"></script>
        <script src="jqueryui/js/jquery-ui-1.8.x.custom.min.js"
type="text/javascript"></script>
        <script src="index.js" type="text/javascript"></script>

    </head>

    <body style="font-size: 10px;">

            <div class="ui-widget">

                    <div class="ui-state-error ui-corner-all"
style="margin-top: 20px; padding: 0 5px; width: 30%;">
                        <p>
                        <span class="ui-icon ui-icon-alert"
style="float: left; margin-right: .3px;"></span>
                        User profile update failed.
                </p>
                    </div>

            </div>

    </body>

</html>
```

2. In the `jqueryui/development-bundle/themes/base` directory, edit the `jquery.ui.theme.css` file.

3. Locate the `.ui-state-error, .ui-widget-content .ui-state-error, .ui-widget-header .ui-state-error` style definition and replace it with the following:

```
.ui-state-error, .ui-widget-content .ui-state-error, .ui-widget-
header .ui-state-error {

    border: 1px solid #cd0a0a;
```

```
background: #fbd5c6;
color: #cd0a0a;
}
```

4. Reload `index.html` in your web browser. You should see something similar to the following:

What just happened?

In `index.html`, we're using the same markup as previous examples in this chapter to display an error message to the user by applying the `ui-state-error` class.

In `jquery.ui.theme.css`, we've updated the `ui-state-error` background style property. We've removed the background image that gives the error state its texture since we only want a solid color. We also save on the HTTP request that is no longer made to the server. We've also changed the background color to be slightly darker.

You'll notice that in the result of these changes made to our theme, the border and font color of the error message might look better if they were slightly darker as well. We haven't changed anything here, as we're only interested in the background style at the moment. However, keep in mind that changes made to the background often result in further modifications to the theme in other areas.

Time for action - accordion error background

Let's see how the changes made to our theme in the previous example look when applied to an accordion section:

1. Edit the `index.html` file created earlier and replace the content with the following:

```html
<html xmlns="http://www.w3.org/1999/xhtml">

    <head>

        <title>Customizing Interaction Cues</title>

        <link href="jqueryui/development-bundle/themes/base/
jquery.ui.all.css" rel="stylesheet" type="text/css" />

        <script src="jqueryui/js/jquery-1.5.x.min.js" type="text/
javascript"></script>
```

```
        <script src="jqueryui/js/jquery-ui-1.8.x.custom.min.js"
type="text/javascript"></script>
        <script src="index.js" type="text/javascript"></script>

    </head>

    <body style="font-size: 10px;">

        <div style="width: 40%;">

            <div id="my_accordion">

                <h3><a href="#">First</a></h3>
                <div>
                    <p>First paragraph</p>
                    <p>Second paragraph</p>
                    <p>Third paragraph</p>
                </div>

                <h3><a href="#">Second</a></h3>
                <div></div>

                <h3><a href="#">Third</a></h3>
                <div></div>

            </div>

        </div>

    </body>

</html>
```

2. Edit the `index.js` file created earlier and replace the content with the following:

```
$(document).ready(function(){

    $("#my_accordion").accordion();
    $("#my_accordion h3:eq(2)").addClass("ui-state-error")

});
```

3. Reuse the changes made to the `jquery.ui.theme.css` file in the previous example. This will preserve the changes made to the `background` property of the `ui-state-error` class.

4. Reload `index.html` in your web browser. You should see something similar to the following:

What just happened?

We've reused the style changes we made to the `ui-state-error` class in the previous example.

In index.html, we've created the markup required for a sample accordion widget. In index.js, we create the jQuery UI accordion widget when the page finishes loading.

Once the accordion is created, we then apply the `ui-state-error` class to the third accordion section.

Error font

The `ui-state-error` class has the potential to affect the appearance of text when applied to certain elements. This could be an error message or a widget component containing text.

Time for action - error message font

It's time to update the `ui-state-error` class in our theme to alter the appearance of text in an error state:

1. Edit the `index.html` file created earlier and replace the content with the following:

```
<html xmlns="http://www.w3.org/1999/xhtml">

    <head>

        <title>Customizing Interaction Cues</title>

        <link href="jqueryui/development-bundle/themes/base/
          jquery.ui.all.css" rel="stylesheet" type="text/css" />
```

```
            <script src="jqueryui/js/jquery-1.5.x.min.js" type="text/
            javascript"></script>
            <script src="jqueryui/js/jquery-ui-1.8.x.custom.min.js"
            type="text/javascript"></script>
            <script src="index.js" type="text/javascript"></script>

    </head>

    <body style="font-size: 10px;">

            <div class="ui-widget">

                    <div class="ui-state-error ui-corner-all"
                    style="margin-top: 20px; padding: 0 5px;
                    width: 30%;">
                            <p>
                    <span class="ui-icon ui-icon-alert"
                    style="float: left; margin-right: .3px;">
                    </span>
                    User profile update failed.
            </p>
                    </div>

            </div>

    </body>

</html>
```

2. In the `jqueryui/development-bundle/themes/base` directory, edit the `jquery.ui.theme.css` file.

3. Locate the `.ui-state-error, .ui-widget-content .ui-state-error, .ui-widget-header .ui-state-error` style definition and replace the content with the following:

```
.ui-state-error, .ui-widget-content .ui-state-error, .ui-widget-
header .ui-state-error {

    border: 1px solid #cd0a0a;
    background: #fef1ec url(images/ui-bg_glass_95_fef1ec_1x400.
    png) 50% 50% repeat-x;
    color: #b90404;
    font-weight: bold;

}
```

3. Reload `index.html` in your web browser. You should see something similar to the following:

What just happened?

We just updated the font style properties of the `ui-state-error` class. The font color is slightly darker than the original font color and the font weight is new bold. This makes the content of the error message really stand out.

Time for action - error button font

Now we can see how the changes we just made to our theme will affect button widgets in an error state:

1. Edit the `index.html` file created earlier and replace the content with the following:

```
<html xmlns="http://www.w3.org/1999/xhtml">

    <head>

        <title>Customizing Interaction Cues</title>

        <link href="jqueryui/development-bundle/themes/base/
          jquery.ui.all.css" rel="stylesheet" type="text/css" />

        <script src="jqueryui/js/jquery-1.5.x.min.js" type="text/
          javascript"></script>
        <script src="jqueryui/js/jquery-ui-1.8.x.custom.min.js"
          type="text/javascript"></script>
        <script src="index.js" type="text/javascript"></script>

    </head>

    <body style="font-size: 10px;">

        <button id="my_button">Click Me</button>

    </body>

</html>
```

2. Edit the `index.js` file created earlier and replace the content with the following:

```
$(document).ready(function(){

    $("#my_button").button().addClass("ui-state-error");

});
```

3. Reuse the changes made to the `jquery.ui.theme.css` file in the previous example. This will preserve the font style properties we've altered.

4. Reload `index.html` in your web browser. You should see something similar to the following:

What just happened?

We've created a button widget and applied the `ui-state-error` class to it. This changes the appearance of the button so that it looks like it was the cause of something failing.

We can also see that the font style properties we changed are also applied here, so the button text in question really stands out.

Pop quiz – the error state

1. When does it make sense to apply the error state?

    a. You apply the error state to to indicate to the user that something went wrong, such as an invalid form entry or the server returned an error.

    b. jQuery UI widgets will automatically apply the error state for you.

    c. Only when there is a Javascript error on the page.

2. Do the error state and the highlight state share any style properties?

    a. The error state and the highlight state use the same properties, but always have different values for those properties because they should look very different from one another.

    b. The error state and the highlight state have nothing in common.

    c. The error state has a different background color from the highlight state.

3. How is the error state applied to jQuery UI widgets?

    a. No jQuery UI widgets will automatically apply the error state – it must be applied by the application to individual widget components such as a tab.

    b. The error state cannot be applied to widgets – only custom error messages.

    c. The error state is applied to jQuery UI widgets by adding the class to the entire widget.

The disabled state

The **disabled state** shows a page element or widget component as 'out of order'. When something in the user interface enters a disabled state, it cues the user to not touch it. For instance, maybe a user doesn't have appropriate permissions to execute some action that would otherwise be made available. Maybe the user is on your site and you want to show the features they would have if they upgraded their account. Or maybe the user needs to complete some action before they can continue, such as clicking on a disclaimer check box before submitting a form.

The key feature of the disabled state is that it allows for user interfaces to display things that would otherwise need to be hidden. If a button, for whatever reason, can't or shouldn't be clicked, the easy solution is to hide it entirely. This isn't optimal, however, because the user might be expecting that button to be there. This could also potentially alter the positioning of other page elements. The alternative, applying the disabled state class from the jQuery UI theming framework, allows us to keep the user interface predictable.

Disabled opacity

A good way to indicate that something in a web user interface is disabled is by decreasing the opacity. The element then fades into the background so to speak. Additionally, users tend to recognize this visual cue as disabled.

Time for action - increasing disabled opacity

We may find that opacity of our theme is too dark. Luckily, we can alter the opacity style property of the disabled state so as to make them a little less transparent:

1. Reuse the changes made to the index.html in the previous example.

2. Edit the `index.js` file created earlier and replace the content with the following:

```
$(document).ready(function(){

    $("#my_button").button().addClass("ui-state-disabled");

});
```

3. In the `jqueryui/development-bundel/themes/base` directory, edit the `jquery.ui.theme.css` file.

4. Locate the `.ui-state-disabled, .ui-widget-content .ui-state-disabled, .ui-widget-header .ui-state-disabled` style definition and replace it with the following:

```
.ui-state-disabled, .ui-widget-content .ui-state-disabled, .ui-widget-header .ui-state-disabled {

    opacity: .45;
    filter:Alpha(Opacity=45);
    background-image: none;

}
```

5. Reload `index.html` in your web browser. You should see something similar to the following:

What just happened?

We've reused the button widget from the previous example. Here, we're applying the disabled state to it. We've also updated the `ui-state-disabled` class to be slightly more opaque. We can see the button a little better, but at the same time, it is still obviously disabled.

 The opacity style property is recognized by all major browsers, aside from IE 8 or earlier.

Have a go hero

In the previous example, we've applied the disabled state to a button widget. The button appears to be disabled, but if the user attempts clicking it, the event will still fire. Try using the following code in conjunction with applying the disabled state to truly disable the button.

```
$("#my_button").button()
.addClass("ui-state-disabled")
.click(function(){return false;});
```

Priorities

Priorities allow us to show the user that within a group of widgets, some take the priority over others. For instance, with a group of five button widgets, two might be more relevant to the user than the other three. We use priorities to cue importance or urgency. There are two types of priorities within the jQuery UI theming framework - primary and secondary. Primary priorities need to make the widget in question stand out relative to the other widgets in the group. The secondary priority is meant to give the appearance of irrelevance.

Time for action - button priorities

Let's make a group of button widgets and give them some priorities:

1. Edit the `index.html` file created earlier and replace the content with the following:

```
<html xmlns="http://www.w3.org/1999/xhtml">

    <head>

        <title>Customizing Interaction Cues</title>

        <link href="jqueryui/development-bundle/themes/base/
          jquery.ui.all.css" rel="stylesheet" type="text/css" />

        <script src="jqueryui/js/jquery-1.5.x.min.js" type="text/
          javascript"></script>
        <script src="jqueryui/js/jquery-ui-1.8.x.custom.min.js"
          type="text/javascript"></script>
        <script src="index.js" type="text/javascript"></script>

    </head>

    <body style="font-size: 10px;">

        <button id="priority_button">Priority Button</button>
        <button id="normal_button">Normal Button</button>
        <button id="secondary_button">Secondary Button</button>

    </body>

</html>
```

2. Edit the `index.js` file created earlier and replace the content with the following:

```
$(document).ready(function(){

    $("#priority_button").button().addClass("ui-priority-
primary");
    $("#normal_button").button()
```

```
        $("#secondary_button").button().addClass("ui-priority-
    secondary");

});
```

3. In the `jqueryui/development-bundle/themes/base` directory, edit the `jquery.ui.theme.css` file.

4. Locate the `.ui-priority-primary, .ui-widget-content .ui-priority-primary, .ui-widget-header .ui-priority-primary` style definition and replace it with the following:

```
.ui-priority-primary, .ui-widget-content .ui-priority-primary,
.ui-widget-header .ui-priority-primary {

    font-weight: bold;
    border: 1px solid #858585;

}
```

5. Locate the `.ui-priority-secondary, .ui-widget-content .ui-priority-secondary, .ui-widget-header .ui-priority-secondary` style definition and replace it with the following:

```
.ui-priority-secondary, .ui-widget-content .ui-priority-secondary,
.ui-widget-header .ui-priority-secondary {

    opacity: .65;
    filter:Alpha(Opacity=65);
    font-weight: normal;

}
```

6. Reload `index.html` in your web browser. You should see something similar to the following:

What just happened?

We've created three `button` elements in `index.html`. In `index.js`, we turn those elements into jQuery UI button widgets when the page has finished loading.

In `jquery.ui.theme.css`, we've updated the `ui-priority-primary` and `ui-priority-secondary` classes. We gave the `ui-priority-primary` class a darker border so as to further emphasize its importance. We made the `ui-priority-secondary` class slightly less opaque so as to further undermine its relevance.

Summary

We've seen in this chapter that the jQuery UI theming framework has a lot to offer when it comes to cuing important information to users. We applications need to display messages to users, informing them of successful and erroneous events. It isn't enough to use the same presentational styles for both cue classes; the difference needs to stand out.

The `ui-state-highlight` and `ui-state-error` classes help us achieve this distinction while looking consistent with the rest of the user interface. This is especially useful in the context of a theme because we can apply these various cue states to widget components as well. We're not just restricted to putting text in an error or highlight state.

Another useful cue we want to give users is that of something being disabled. It is better than hiding these elements from the user interface entirely, as this can be misleading. Finally, we've seen that we can also give the user a sense of urgency within a group of widgets by applying priority cue classes.

Now that you've got a firm understanding of interaction cues, it's time to move on to more specialized jQuery UI theme topics. Up until this point, we've covered the essential CSS classes of the theme framework. In the next chapter, we'll explore using icons in themes. We'll look at using icons that ship with the framework, as well as extending the icon set with our own.

7
Creating Theme Icons

Icons inform users as to what something does. Icons also need to belong as part of the overall look and feel of the theme.

In this chapter we shall:

◆ Look at the role icons play in themes

◆ Use icons with states

◆ Create theme icon sets

◆ Extend existing icon sets

So let's get on with it.

What are theme icons?

In any user interface, we see icons all over the place. On your desktop, you see icons that represent the various application shortcuts as well as any files you've placed there. The window containing your web browser has icons for the maximize, minimize, and close actions. The benefit of using icons is that they're incredibly space-efficient, as long as they're descriptive. Using icons out of context defeats their purpose - you don't want a button with a "down arrow" icon in your toolbar. This doesn't mean anything to the user. Having a button with a "trashcan" icon in the tool-bar does make sense—it means I want to delete what I'm looking at. Another potentially harmful use is using icons in places where a text description would better inform the user. For instance, displaying a "trashcan" button in the toolbar might confuse the user if there are several things displayed on the same page, even if they've selected something. In these scenarios, we're often better off using a combination of text and an icon.

The jQuery UI theming framework provides a large selection of icons we can use in our user interfaces. Some of these icons are already used in some widgets, for instance, the accordion uses arrow icons by default. Not only are the icon graphics provided to us - we can choose icon colors in the ThemRoller application - but we also have powerful CSS class we use to apply the icons. Using these classes, we can give existing jQuery UI widgets new icons or we can place them strategically in our application user interface where they prove helpful.

Sometimes, the provided icon set will only go so far. You'll find that at one point or another, you need new icons that better reflect the concepts of your application domain. Throughout the remainder of this chapter, we'll look at how theme icons work with jQuery UI widgets, how we can use them independently, and how we can build our own icons.

Time for action - preparing the example

It's time to set up an environment for examples throughout the remainder of this chapter. As mentioned in the previous chapter, it is best that you restore the state of your example environment using the steps here. This only applies if you've been following examples from previous chapters:

1. If you haven't already, download and extract the jQuery UI package into a directory called jQuery UI from `http://jqueryui.com/download`.

2. At the same level as the jQuery UI directory, create a new `index.html` file with the following content:

```
<html xmlns="http://www.w3.org/1999/xhtml">

    <head>

        <title>Creating Theme Icons</title>

        <link href="jqueryui/development-bundle/themes/base/
jquery.ui.all.css" rel="stylesheet" type="text/css" />

        <script src="jqueryui/js/jquery-1.5.x.min.js" type="text/
javascript"></script>
        <script src="jqueryui/js/jquery-ui-1.8.x.custom.min.js"
type="text/javascript"></script>
        <script src="index.js" type="text/javascript"></script>

    </head>

    <body style="font-size: 10px;">

        <button id="my_button">Click Me</button>

    </body>

</html>
```

3. At the same level as the `jqueryui` directory, create a new `index.js` file with the following content.

```
$(document).ready(function(){

    $("#my_button").button();

});
```

4. Open `index.html` in your web browser; you should see something similar to the following:

Icons in widgets

Several jQuery UI widgets have icons from the theming framework embedded inside them. We use icons inside widgets to decorate them and to add meaning. Icons are similar to interaction cues, which we saw in the previous chapter—they help guide the user through the application workflow by given subtle hints. Before we start modifying icons used in our theme, we need to take a closer look at the role they play in widgets.

Time for action - default widget icons

Let's take a look at some of the icons displayed in jQuery UI widgets by default:

1. Edit the `index.html` file created earlier and replace the content with the following:

```
<html xmlns="http://www.w3.org/1999/xhtml">

    <head>

        <title>Creating Theme Icons</title>

        <link href="jqueryui/development-bundle/themes/base/
jquery.ui.all.css" rel="stylesheet" type="text/css" />

        <script src="jqueryui/js/jquery-1.5.x.min.js" type="text/
javascript"></script>
        <script src="jqueryui/js/jquery-ui-1.8.x.custom.min.js"
type="text/javascript"></script>
        <script src="index.js" type="text/javascript"></script>

    </head>
```

```html
<body style="font-size: 10px;">

    <input id="my_datepicker" type="text" style="margin-
bottom: 170px;"/>

    <div style="width: 40%;">

        <div id="my_accordion">

            <h3><a href="#">First</a></h3>
            <div>
                <p>First paragraph</p>
                <p>Second paragraph</p>
                <p>Third paragraph</p>
            </div>

            <h3><a href="#">Second</a></h3>
            <div></div>

            <h3><a href="#">Third</a></h3>
            <div></div>

        </div>

    </div>

</body>

</html>
```

2. Edit the `index.js` file created earlier and replace the content with the following:

```js
$(document).ready(function(){

    $("#my_accordion").accordion();
    $("#my_datepicker").datepicker();

});
```

3. Reload `index.html` in your web browser. You should see something similar to the following:

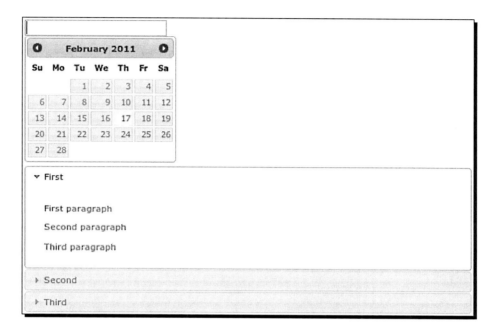

What just happened?

We've just created two widgets—a date-picker and an accordion. In `index.html`, we've created the markup for both widgets and in `index.js`, we construct the jQuery UI components when the page has finished loading.

You'll notice that both widgets have icons in them by default. The date-picker widget has two arrows beside the month and year. The accordion widget has an arrow in each accordion section header.

These widgets have icons by default because they help bring meaning to the widget succinctly. As a user, I can easily deduce the meaning of the arrows in the date-picker: move to the next or previous month. Additionally, the text "Next" and "Previous" are added to their respective icons as titles. An alternate presentation of these controls is a text link or button: "next month", "previous month". This doesn't add any value; it only takes away from the space inside the widget.

The arrow icon role in the accordion widget is even more obvious. The down arrow represents the currently expanded accordion section. The right arrows represent collapsed sections. Without these arrows, the user would eventually figure out how to work the accordion controls; however, the icons make it much more obvious in a non-intrusive way.

Time for action - setting widget icons

In addition to using the default icons in widgets, we have the option to set the icon in certain widgets. Let's see how this is done:

1. Edit the `index.html` file created earlier and replace the content with the following:

```
<html xmlns="http://www.w3.org/1999/xhtml">

    <head>

        <title>Creating Theme Icons</title>

        <link href="jqueryui/development-bundle/themes/base/
         jquery.ui.all.css" rel="stylesheet" type="text/css" />

        <script src="jqueryui/js/jquery-1.5.x.min.js" type="text/
         javascript"></script>
        <script src="jqueryui/js/jquery-ui-1.8.x.custom.min.js"
         type="text/javascript"></script>
        <script src="index.js" type="text/javascript"></script>

    </head>

    <body style="font-size: 10px;">

        <button id="my_button" style="margin-bottom: 10px;">View</
        button>

        <div style="width: 40%;">

            <div id="my_accordion">
                <h3><a href="#">First</a></h3>
                <div>
                    <p>First paragraph</p>
                    <p>Second paragraph</p>
                    <p>Third paragraph</p>
                </div>

                <h3><a href="#">Second</a></h3>
                <div></div>

                <h3><a href="#">Third</a></h3>
                <div></div>

            </div>

        </div>

    </body>

</html>
```

2. Edit the `index.js` file created earlier and replace the content with the following:

```
$(document).ready(function(){

    $("#my_button").button({icons: {primary: "ui-icon-video"}});
    $("#my_accordion").accordion({icons: {header: "ui-icon-circle-
      triangle-e",
    headerSelected: "ui-icon-circle-triangle-s"}
    });

});
```

3. Reload `index.html` in your web browser. You should see something similar to the following:

What just happened?

In `index.html`, we've created a button and an accordion widget. In `index.js`, we build the jQuery UI components of these widgets when the page has finished loading.

In the constructor of the button widget, we pass an object to the `icons` parameter. This object has a `primary` value of `ui-icon-video`. This will give our button a small video icon to the left of the text. Likewise, we pass an object to the icon's parameter in the accordion constructor. This object has two values - `header` has a value of `ui-icon-circle-triangle-e` and `headerSelected` has a value of `ui-icon-circle-triangle-s`.

 The jQuery UI theme framework has several arrow icons to choose from. The framework uses the "compass notation" for arrow icon classes. Say you want an arrow that points up. You could use `ui-icon-circle-triangle-n`, as this arrow points "north".

The button widget has built-in support for adding a button to text in order to provide additional meaning. In our example, the text view isn't very meaningful to the user.

With the video icon beside the text view, it becomes very obvious what the button does.

What we've done with the accordion widget is slightly different. The accordion widget displays icons by default; we've just specified different ones. This is a pure embellishment of the accordion - we've found icons that we'd like to use and replaced the default ones. We might even want to replace them with our own icons that we create. We will see more on this later in the chapter.

Standalone icons

With the jQuery UI theming framework, we're not restricted to applying icon styles, which actually display the icon in the user interface, to widgets. We can apply icon classes to any other page elements where they help illustrate the meaning. It is best to use icons from the same set so that we can preserve consistency.

Time for action - displaying the current user

It's time to place an icon beside the currently logged-in user:

1. Edit the `index.html` file created earlier and replace the content with the following:

    ```html
    <html xmlns="http://www.w3.org/1999/xhtml">

        <head>

            <title>Creating Theme Icons</title>

            <link href="jqueryui/development-bundle/themes/base/
    jquery.ui.all.css" rel="stylesheet" type="text/css" />

            <script src="jqueryui/js/jquery-1.5x.min.js" type="text/
    javascript"></script>
            <script src="jqueryui/js/jquery-ui-1.8.x.custom.min.js"
    type="text/javascript"></script>
            <script src="index.js" type="text/javascript"></script>

        </head>

        <body style="font-size: 10px;">

            <div class="ui-widget ui-widget-content ui-state-default"
    style="width: 30%; padding: 3px;">

                <span class="ui-icon ui-icon-person" style="float:
    left;"></span>
    ```

```
            <span style="margin-left: .3em;">admin</span>
            <span style="float: right;">Last Login: <strong>Feb 23
2011 03:16 PM</strong></span>

        </div>

    </body>

</html>
```

2. Reload `index.html` in your web browser. You should see something similar to the following:

What just happened?

We've created a content box for our user interface which displays the current user and the last time they logged in. In `index.html`, we've created a container `div` element for our user content. This `div` has the `ui-widget`, `ui-widget-content`, and `ui-state-default` classes applied to it. These classes give our content box styles from the jQuery UI theme.

Inside the `div`, we have three span elements. The first span is used to display the user icon. This is done by applying the `ui-icon` and `ui-icon-person` classes to it. The next span displays the current user. Finally, the last span displays the date of the user's previous login.

We call this approach to using icons from the jQuery UI theme "stand-alone" because we're not selecting an icon to display inside a widget as we did in the previous section. Instead, we're applying various constructs from the theming framework, including the icon, to create our own content. As this context box is likely to be of value on more than one page in our application, we'd probably want to create a widget that applies the styles as we've done here. We'll take a closer look at how this is done in the last chapter.

Time for action - identifying entities

In the previous example, we used an icon from the theming framework to identify the current user. We can also use icons to identify groups of different entity types:

1. Edit the `index.html` file created earlier and replace the content with the following:

```
<html xmlns="http://www.w3.org/1999/xhtml">

    <head>
```

```
        <title>Creating Theme Icons</title>

        <link href="jqueryui/development-bundle/themes/base/
jquery.ui.all.css" rel="stylesheet" type="text/css" />

        <script src="jqueryui/js/jquery-1.5.x.min.js" type="text/
javascript"></script>
        <script src="jqueryui/js/jquery-ui-1.8.x.custom.min.js"
type="text/javascript"></script>
        <script src="index.js" type="text/javascript"></script>

        <style type="text/css">

        ul {

            list-style-type: none;
            padding: 1px;

        }

        div, ul li {

            margin-bottom: 2px;

        }

        div {

            width: 30%;
            padding: 3px;

        }

        </style>

    </head>

    <body style="font-size: 10px;">

        <div class="ui-widget ui-widget-content">

            <h1 class="ui-widget ui-widget-header">Unread
Messages</h1>

            <ul>

                <li class="ui-widget ui-widget-content ui-state-
default">

                    <span class="ui-icon ui-icon-mail-closed"
style="float: left;"></span>
```

```
                <span style="margin-left: .3em;">Message 1 -
<i>Subject 1</i></span>

                </li>

                <li class="ui-widget ui-widget-content ui-state-
default">

                        <span class="ui-icon ui-icon-mail-closed"
style="float: left;"></span>
                        <span style="margin-left: .3em;">Message 2 -
<i>Subject 2</i></span>

                </li>

        </ul>

    </div>

    <div class="ui-widget ui-widget-content">

        <h1 class="ui-widget ui-widget-header">Read Messages</
h1>

        <ul>

                <li class="ui-widget ui-widget-content ui-state-
default">

                        <span class="ui-icon ui-icon-mail-open"
style="float: left;"></span>
                        <span style="margin-left: .3em;">Message 3 -
<i>Subject 3</i></span>

                </li>

                <li class="ui-widget ui-widget-content ui-state-
default">

                        <span class="ui-icon ui-icon-mail-open"
style="float: left;"></span>
                        <span style="margin-left: .3em;">Message 4 -
<i>Subject 4</i></span>

                </li>

        </ul>

    </div>

    </body>

</html>
```

2. Reload `index.html` in your web browser. You should see something similar to the following:

Unread Messages

☑ Message 1 - *Subject 1*
☑ Message 2 - *Subject 2*

Read Messages

✉ Message 3 - *Subject 3*
✉ Message 4 - *Subject 4*

What just happened?

We've created two lists—a list of unread messages and a list of read messages. We use an icon to differentiate between the items in each list - a read message and an unread message.

In `index.html`, we have two `div` elements that are nearly identical. We'll explore only one, and then we'll look at the differences. In the header of `index.html`, we've created several style definitions for the purposes of this example. Mostly just padding and removing the default list styles. Within the `div`, we have a h1 header which gives the title of the list. Next, we have the list itself. Each list item has styles from the theming framework applied to it, including the icon that identifies the entity type.

The main difference between the two lists is the entity type. The first list shows unread messages and the second, read messages. We use an icon for each item in the list - `ui-icon-mail-closed` and `ui-icon-main-open`. Sometimes it is valuable to be explicit in what you're labeling with an icon. For instance, we could have just placed the `ui-icon-mail-closed` icon beside the "Unread" header. This would carry the same meaning, just not the same immediacy.

We can use icons to differentiate between the entities in our application. We have the flexibility of applying icons using CSS classes from the theming framework. However, the icon sets provided by default probably won't cover all entities we'll want to display. We'll revisit this limitation later in the chapter.

Icon states

As we've seen previously, jQuery UI widgets change appearance depending on what state they're currently in. For instance, a button in an error state looks different than a button in a default state. Icons in jQuery UI themes also need to change appearance when a change in state is applied. This usually results in the icon changing color. In this section, we'll take a closer look at how states in the CSS framework change the appearance of theme icons.

Time for action - default icons

It's time to see how icons in the default state are applied:

1. Edit the `index.html` file created earlier and replace the content with the following:

```
<html xmlns="http://www.w3.org/1999/xhtml">

    <head>

        <title>Creating Theme Icons</title>

        <link href="jqueryui/development-bundle/themes/base/
jquery.ui.all.css" rel="stylesheet" type="text/css" />

        <script src="jqueryui/js/jquery-1.5.x.min.js" type="text/
javascript"></script>
        <script src="jqueryui/js/jquery-ui-1.8.x.custom.min.js"
type="text/javascript"></script>
        <script src="index.js" type="text/javascript"></script>

    </head>

    <body style="font-size: 10px;">

        <button id="my_button">View</button>

    </body>

</html>
```

2. Edit the `index.js` file created earlier and replace the content with the following:

```
$(document).ready(function(){

    $("#my_button").button({icons: {primary: "ui-icon-video"}});

});
```

3. Reload `index.html` in your web browser. You should see something similar to the following:

What just happened?

We've created a simple button widget. In `index.html`, we've got a basic button element that is transformed into a jQuery UI button widget in `index.js` when the page has finished loading. We specify the icon we want to use in the button's constructor.

This button is in a default state. This means that the `.ui-state-default` `.ui-icon` `style` definition determines the icon image file used on the button. The following diagram illustrates how the image file is selected:

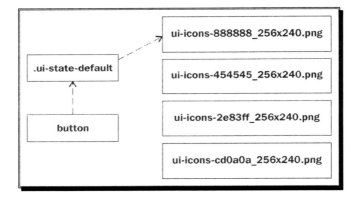

Time for action - highlight icons

It's time to see how icons in the highlight state are applied:

1. Reuse the same content from `index.html` in the previous example.

2. Edit the `index.js` file created earlier and replace the content with the following:

```
$(document).ready(function(){

    $("#my_button").button({icons: {primary: "ui-icon-video"}})
                   .addClass('ui-state-highlight');

});
```

3. Reload `index.html` in your web browser. You should see something similar to the following:

What just happened?

We've reused the same HTML from the previous example to create a button that has a video icon in it. In `index.js`, once the jQuery UI button is constructed, we apply the `ui-state-highlight` class to it. This changes the image file used to display the icon in the button. The following illustration depicts how the `.ui-state-highlight .ui-icon` style definition applies the appropriate image file to the button:

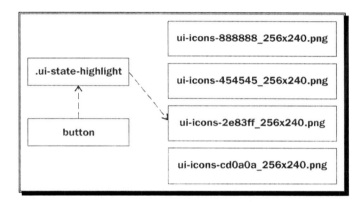

Time for action - error icons

It's time to see how icons in the error state are applied:

1. Reuse the same content from `index.html` in the previous example.

2. Edit the `index.js` file created earlier and replace the content with the following:

```
$(document).ready(function(){

    $("#my_button").button({icons: {primary: "ui-icon-video"}})
                   .addClass('ui-state-error');

});
```

3. Reload `index.html` in your web browser. You should see something similar to the following:

What just happened?

We've replicated the previous example with one minor difference - the button is now in an error state instead of a highlight state. This also changes the color of the icon displayed in the button to read. This obviously wouldn't look right had the button icon kept the default color.

The icon in the button uses the `.ui-state-error .ui-icon, .ui-state-error-text .ui-icon` style definition to apply the icon image file. The following illustration shows how the button widget acquires the image file based on its state:

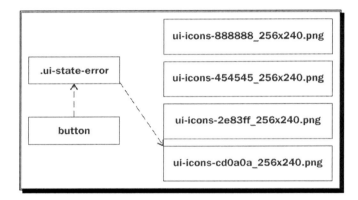

Time for action - hover icons

It's time to see how icons are applied to buttons in a hover state:

1. Reuse the content from `index.html` in the previous example.

2. Edit the `index.html` file created earlier and replace it with the following:

```
$(document).ready(function(){

    $("#my_button").button({icons: {primary: "ui-icon-video"}});

});
```

3. Reload `index.html` in your web browser and hover over the button. You should see something similar to the following:

What just happened?

We created a plain jQuery UI button widget. This button is in a default state. We put it into a hover state moving the mouse pointer over it. When we put the button into a hover state, we're actually changing the button's icon image. This is due to the `ui-state-hover .ui-icon, .ui-state-focus .ui-icon` style selector. The image file used when the button enters the hover state is illustrated as follows:

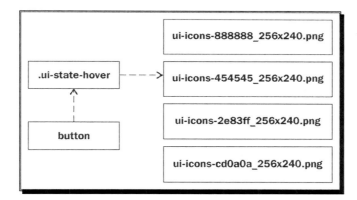

Have a go hero

Try updating the `ui-state-hover` class in the theme CSS so that it points to a different image file.

Sprites

Until this point in the chapter, we haven't made any changes to our themes. We've walked through some examples to get a better feel for how theme icons work when applied to widgets, or used outside of widgets. We've seen how different icon images are used depending what state the icon is in.

We're now going to take a closer look at what these icon images contain. Each icon image file in a jQuery UI theme uses a sprite to differentiate between the different icons in the set.

What are sprites?

A **sprite** is a concept used to store several smaller images in a single image file. A single image is composed of a grid, each cell representing a smaller image. However, only one grid cell is ever displayed in the user interface at one point in time. The grid of smaller images is the sprite map while each cell is a sprite. The following illustration gives us an idea of how sprite maps are broken down into cellular components:

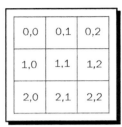

Here, we have a simple representation of a sprite image. This simple grid gives us an easy coordinate system we use to specify the active cell. In the case of a jQuery UI icon file, the CSS class translates into a coordinate in the sprite. For example, imagine that the trash icon we want to display in our user interface is located in the middle of our sample layout about, 1,1. The CSS class for that icon, ui-icon-trash, knows that it is located at 1,1.

The icon classes of the theme framework have styles associated with them that use the position of the sprite – the width and height – to set the background-position, width, and height properties of the HTML container. The alternative is to have each icon stored in an individual file. This, however, presents a multitude of problems - overhead with HTTP requests for retrieving the icons to display, the complexity of maintaining a theme with that many files. The sprite solution to the problem of icons as part of a theme is an elegant one - there are only a handful of image files to maintain and there is relatively little overhead.

At first glance, referencing individual icons by a pair of integer coordinates doesn't seem like an ideal way to reference icons. We can, however, group our icons into logical categories within the sprite.

Icon categories

Logical categories within jQuery UI icon sprites are divided into rows. Each row represents a distinct concept, like arrows or file types. The default icon sets provided in jQuery UI themes group icons using this approach. You'll notice two things about the default icon layout in the image files if you open it for a closer look. First, related icons are displayed on the same row. Second, not all rows are the same length. This means that some icon categories have more icons than others. At the same time, we don't want to have really long rows of icons, as this just leads to larger images due to wasted space. Instead, it makes more sense to have larger icon categories wrap to another row.

Theme icon sets

Now that we have a firm understanding of how theme icons work in jQuery UI, and we understand how icon sprites work within the framework, it's time to create some icons of our own.

As we've seen throughout the previous chapters in this book, the jQuery UI theme framework puts a large emphasis on providing a consistent look and feel. You can tell that two widgets, a date-picker and a progress bar for example, belong to the same theme. The same is true of theme icons in the framework. The same set of icons exists in all themes. When extending the theme icons, it is best to be conservative. Chances are there that there is an icon that can already represent what you're looking for. The "less is more" principle is especially fruitful when it comes to managing theme icons.

The examples in this section use the **GIMP (GNU Image Manipulation Tool)** for modifying the jQuery UI icon sprites. GIMP is freely available at `http://www.gimp.org/` and runs on all major operating systems. Although no prior knowledge of this tool is required for the examples here, there are plenty of resources available online.

Time for action - creating new icons

It's now time for us to create new icons for our theme. The first step is to update the sprite image files. The second step is to add new icon classes to the theme CSS.

For this example, I'm adding one new icon to my theme. I need a new simple shape - a diamond. This new icon is illustrated as follows:

You can use any image you like for this example. The only restrictions are that the image needs have a dimension of 16x16 pixels:

1. Open **GIMP** and create a new image by selecting **File | New** as illustrated in the following screenshot:

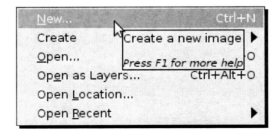

2. In the new image dialog, set the image dimensions to a width of 256 pixels and a height of 256 pixels as illustrated in the following screenshot:

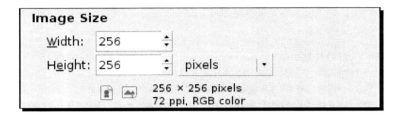

3. If the Layers dialog isn't open already, open it by selecting **Windows | Dockable Dialogs | Layers** as illustrated in the following screenshot:

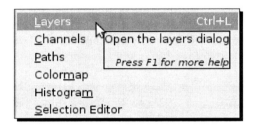

4. In the **Layers** dialog, make the **Background** layer transparent by clicking the eyeball icon as illustrated in the following screenshot:

5. Open the `jqueryui/development-bundle/themes/base/images/ui-icons_2e83ff_256x240.png` file as a layer. The following screenshots illustrate how this is done:

We can see here the selected layer that we just opened:

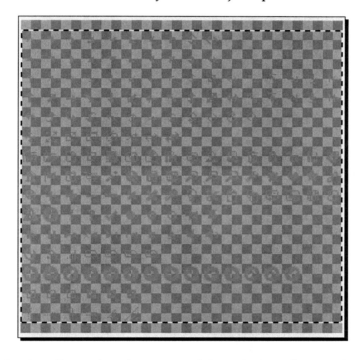

6. In the GIMP toolbox, select the *move* tool. Drag the icons layer to the top of the image. This will leave a row at the bottom of the image with a height of 16 pixels. This is where our new icon is going to be placed:

We can see here there isn't any empty space above the icons layer once we've moved it:

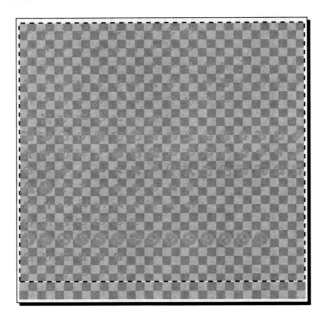

7. Open the image for the file icon you're adding to the set. Select the *move* tool and place at the bottom left of the image sprite illustrated as follows:

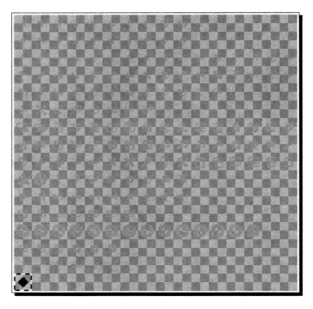

8. In the GIMP toolbox, select the color picker tool. Select the color from one of the existing icons. This will set the active foreground color illustrated as follows:

We can see here that we've changed the foreground color:

9. In the GIMP toolbox, select the bucket fill tool. Move the pointer over the diamond icon and left-click. This will change the color of the icon to match the rest of the set illustrated as follows:

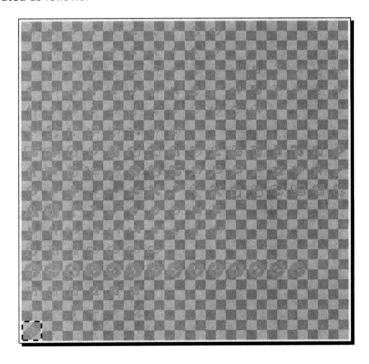

10. Save the image as `jqueryui/development-bundle/themes/base/images/ui-icons_2e83ff_256x256.png`.

11 Repeat the process for the remaining theme icon sprites (optional).

12. Edit the `jqueryui/development-bundle/themes/base/jquery.ui.theme.css` file.

13. Replace the icon state classes that load the icon image files with the following:

```
.ui-icon { width: 16px; height: 16px; background-image:
url(images/ui-icons_222222_256x256.png)/*{iconsContent}*/; }
.ui-widget-content .ui-icon {background-image: url(images/ui-
icons_222222_256x256.png)/*{iconsContent}*/; }
.ui-widget-header .ui-icon {background-image: url(images/ui-
icons_222222_256x256.png)/*{iconsHeader}*/; }
.ui-state-default .ui-icon { background-image: url(images/ui-
icons_888888_256x256.png)/*{iconsDefault}*/; }
.ui-state-hover .ui-icon, .ui-state-focus .ui-icon {background-
image: url(images/ui-icons_454545_256x256.png)/*{iconsHover}*/; }
.ui-state-active .ui-icon {background-image: url(images/ui-
icons_454545_256x256.png)/*{iconsActive}*/; }
.ui-state-highlight .ui-icon {background-image: url(images/ui-
icons_2e83ff_256x256.png)/*{iconsHighlight}*/; }
.ui-state-error .ui-icon, .ui-state-error-text .ui-icon
{background-image: url(images/ui-icons_cd0a0a_256x256.
png)/*{iconsError}*/; }
```

14. At the end of the specific icon position classes, add the following:

```
.ui-icon-diamond { background-position: 0 -240px; }
```

15. Edit the `index.html` file created earlier and replace the content with the following:

```
<html xmlns="http://www.w3.org/1999/xhtml">

    <head>

        <title>Creating Theme Icons</title>

        <link href="jqueryui/development-bundle/themes/base/
jquery.ui.all.css" rel="stylesheet" type="text/css" />

        <script src="jqueryui/js/jquery-1.5.x.min.js" type="text/
javascript"></script>
        <script src="jqueryui/js/jquery-ui-1.8.x.custom.min.js"
type="text/javascript"></script>
        <script src="index.js" type="text/javascript"></script>

    </head>
```

```
<body style="font-size: 10px;">

    <button id="default_button">Default</button>
    <button id="highlight_button">Highlight</button>
    <button id="error_button">Error</button>

</body>

</html>
```

16. Edit the `index.js` file created earlier and replace the content with the following:

```
$(document).ready(function(){

    $("#default_button").button({icons: {primary: "ui-icon-
diamond"}});
    $("#highlight_button").button({icons: {primary: "ui-icon-
diamond"}}).addClass('ui-state-highlight');
    $("#error_button").button({icons: {primary: "ui-icon-
diamond"}}).addClass('ui-state-error');

});
```

17. Reload `index.html` in your web browser. You should see something similar to the following:

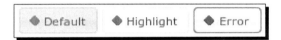

What just happened?

We've just extended the jQuery UI default theme icon set with our own icon. The bulk of the work was modifying the sprite image files using the GIMP tool. The remainder of the changes involved changing the image file names loaded in the CSS icon state classes, and adding a new icon class to load our specific state.

In `index.html` and `index.js`, we create three jQuery UI button widgets to show off our new icon.

Pop quiz – creating theme icons

1. How are theme icons stored in image files?

   a. Theme icons are stored in a single image file as a "sprite map" - each icon is a "sprite".

   b. Each theme icon is stored in its own file.

   c. It is up to the theme author to decide how to store icon images as there is no standard.

2. Do icon image files need to support transparent backgrounds?

   a. Icon image files need to support transparent backgrounds so that they can be used inside widgets.

   b. Icon image files do not require transparent backgrounds.

   c. Only certain icons require transparent backgrounds.

3. How does the theme CSS framework know how to use new icon images?

   a. The author of the new icon needs to update the theme CSS by adding a new class that points to the icon position in the sprite map. This new class can then be used to insert the icon into user interfaces.

   b. New icons are automatically detected by the framework, based of the size of the image file.

   c. New icons are inserted into user interfaces with JavaScript.

Summary

We've learned a lot about jQuery UI theme icons in this chapter. We've also learned about the roles icons play in user interfaces. Icons are most effective when they add meaning to user interface components, and as a side-effect, reduce the amount of redundant text.

The jQuery UI theming framework allows icons to be used both in widgets as well as being placed on the page as stand-alone elements. Different icon images files are used depending on the state of the icon. This is made possible by using a sprite technique to arrange icons. The only difference between the image files is their colors.

Finally, we walked through the process of extending an icon set with our own icons. This is fairly easy to do with a graphical editor such as GIMP.

Now that we're jQuery UI theme icon experts, it's time to add some special effects.

8
Special Effects

There is more to a theme than simple colors, shapes, and sizes. We can do a lot to spice up our themes with special effects found in the jQuery UI theming framework.

In this chapter, we shall:

- Define widget corners
- Use an overlay
- Work with shadows
- Theme standard HTML elements
- Discuss theme positioning and alignment

So let's get on with it.

Setting up a jQuery environment

It is time to set up an environment for examples throughout the remainder of this chapter. As mentioned in the previous chapter, it is best that you restore the state of your example environment using the steps here. This only applies if you've been following examples from previous chapters:

1. If you haven't already, download and extract the jQuery UI package into a directory called jQuery UI from `http://jqueryui.com/download`.

2. At the same level as the jQuery UI directory, create a new `index.html` file with the following content:

```
<html xmlns="http://www.w3.org/1999/xhtml">

    <head>

        <title>Customizing Interaction Cues</title>

        <link href="jqueryui/development-bundle/themes/base/
         jquery.ui.all.css" rel="stylesheet" type="text/css" />

        <script src="jqueryui/js/jquery-1.5.x.min.js" type="text/
         javascript"></script>
        <script src="jqueryui/js/jquery-ui-1.8.x.custom.min.js"
         type="text/javascript"></script>
        <script src="index.js" type="text/javascript"></script>

    </head>

    <body style="font-size: 10px;">

        <button id="my_button">Click Me</button>

    </body>

</html>
```

3. At the same level as the jQuery UI directory, create a new `index.js` file with the following content:

```
$(document).ready(function(){

    $("#my_button").button();

});
```

4. Open `index.html` in your web browser; you should see something similar to the following screenshot:

Theme corners

You've probably noticed that a lot of websites these days use rounded corners in their styles. For example, a login box containing inputs for a username and password and a login button, is rectangular in shape. However, instead of having straight corners with right angles, these rectangular boxes will have slightly rounded corners.

The login box is a simple, but common example of compartmentalized content we apply styles to as user interface designers. We want each one of these components to share the same theme and to look professionally polished. Rounded corners are a simple way to up the aesthetic appeal of your web site. However, it hasn't always been so simple to do. Luckily, jQuery UI themes provide us with the necessary tools to apply corner styles to our widget components in a theme-friendly way.

The legacy approach

The legacy approach to applying rounded corners to page elements involved using images to give the appearance of being round. These aren't corners at all - we're using background images to give the illusion of having round corners. The content elements we want to apply round corners to, used either a single background image or several images - one for each corner of the element. As with anything in software development, there were benefits and repercussions to this approach.

The benefit of using images to give the appearance of having rounded corners on an HTML element is that we can completely control our style within an image. We the controls of a graphics application to dictate the degree of roundness - very round, slightly round, or something in between. We can also control the color and texture of the background using an image, including the corners. But this isn't necessarily a good thing.

Using images to completely control the design of content elements on your website means you're moving outside the design tools at your disposal - CSS. What this means is that using background images to try to give an appearance of round edges on any page element doesn't fit in either HTML or CSS standards - they're a hack. Besides complying with standards, using images means added server resources that need to be downloaded by the web browser.

 There is now a new approach that uses CSS styles to add rounded edges to your user interfaces. This is the approach jQuery UI themes employ. Though not perfectly standardized, they avoid using background images to specify HTML element shapes and is the next step in the right direction.

The style approach

With the advent of CSS3, we now have the `border-radius` style property at our disposal. This property, when set to true, defines the corner roundness of elements to which the style is applied to. The `border-radius` property determines the roundness of all four corners. Like the `border` property, we can also set the roundness of individual corners. For instance, if we only wanted rounded corners on the top of our element, we could set the `border-top-left-radius` and `border-top-right-radius` properties.

So how do we dictate the corner roundness of an HTML element using radii? The best way to visualize this is to think of a circle being placed in the corner of your element. The size of the circle is based on the supplied radius value. Say I use the following style property in one of my CSS classes - `border-top-left-radius: 10px`. The circle used to generate the corner can be visualized below:

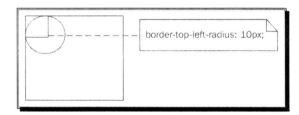

As we can see here, the radius determines the roundness of the element corner by changing the size of the circle. If the radius were smaller, our element corner would be less rounded. Here is what our resulting HTML element might look like:

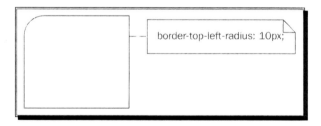

Using CSS styles to set the roundness of elements solves some of the problems inherent with the legacy approach of using images as a corner facade. Problems with using images for rounded corners include:

◆ Corner images need to be maintained. This means that if the website design changes, all corner images need to be updated too.

◆ Applications that use corner images consume more bandwidth as each image needs to be downloaded by the browser.

◆ The selling point for using CSS to design your rounded corners is that this approach doesn't involve using any images. The maintenance costs are restricted to CSS – typically a single class. There are, however, a few caveats to be aware of when using CSS for rounded corners:

    ❏ Images look and behave the same across all browser platforms. You can never be 100% sure with how your corners will look in different browsers using CSS alone.

The border-radius property used to give corners their roundness isn't fully supported by all browsers at the time of this writing. For instance, you'll sometimes see a `-moz` or a `-webkit` prefix on the various `border-radius` properties. At first glance, it might seem as though the CSS approach isn't so maintenance-friendly. Luckily, we can use the jQuery UI theming framework to add an abstraction layer on top of these browser support issues, and to add a couple of useful tools too.

Pop quiz – theme corners

1. How are images used to give page elements the appearance of having rounded corners?

    a. The image itself contains a rounded shape. The image is then placed near the corner of the element.

    b. Images contain a transparent section where the rounded corner should be placed.

    c. Images cannot be used to give the appearance of having rounded corners.

2. How does the `border-radius` property define the roundness of a corner?

    a. The value of the `border-radius` property dictates the size of the imaginary circle placed in the corner of the element. This circle, in turn, determines the roundness of the corner.

    b. The `border-radius` property defines the roundness of corners by giving the value of an arc.

    c. The `border-radius` property doesn't set the roundness of corners.

3. What are some of the benefits to using CSS for rounded corners instead of using images?

    a. The CSS approach to rounded corners doesn't involve using images. This simplifies the task of maintaining a user interface and improves performance.

    b. The CSS approach to rounded corners makes it easier to use corner images.

    c. The CSS approach to rounded corners is inferior to the image-based approach.

The jQuery UI approach

Now that we've seen how to apply rounded corners using both the legacy approach of applying corner images to elements and the newer CSS approach of using the border-radius properties, it's time to see how rounded borders are used in the jQuery UI theming framework.

Time for action - setting all corners

We're now going to create an HTML element and use CSS classes from the jQuery UI theme framework to set the border styles:

1. Edit the index.html file created earlier and replace the content with the following:

```
<html xmlns="http://www.w3.org/1999/xhtml">

    <head>

        <title>Special Effects</title>

        <link href="jqueryui/development-bundle/themes/base/
          jquery.ui.all.css" rel="stylesheet" type="text/css" />

        <script src="jqueryui/js/jquery-1.5.x.min.js" type="text/
          javascript"></script>
        <script src="jqueryui/js/jquery-ui-1.8.x.custom.min.js"
          type="text/javascript"></script>
        <script src="index.js" type="text/javascript"></script>

    </head>

    <body style="font-size: 10px;">

        <div class="ui-widget ui-widget-content ui-state-default
          ui-corner-all" style="width: 25%;">

            <p style="text-align: center;">My Rounded Corners</p>

        </div>

    </body>

</html>
```

2. Reload `index.html` in your web browser. You should see something similar to the following screenshot:

What just happened?

In `index.html`, we've created a basic `div` element with some content and applied rounded corners to it. There is a lot going on in the class attribute of the `div`. The first three classes, `ui-widget`, `ui-widget-content`, and `ui-state-default` simply give the element some theme style properties such as font, border, and background. The fourth class, `ui-corner-all`, is what gives our element its rounded corners.

This class ensures that the rounded corners work in all major web browsers. It does so by using all known prefixes for the `border-radius` style properties. It also uses the standardized `border-radius` property, without any prefix, so that if the browser supports it, this will be used instead.

Time for action - setting top corners

In the previous example, we set all four corners of our element. Now, we're going to set only the two top corners:

1. Edit the `index.html` file created earlier and replace the content with the following:

```
<html xmlns="http://www.w3.org/1999/xhtml">

    <head>

        <title>Special Effects</title>

        <link href="jqueryui/development-bundle/themes/base/
         jquery.ui.all.css" rel="stylesheet" type="text/css" />

        <script src="jqueryui/js/jquery-1.5.x.min.js" type="text/
         javascript"></script>
        <script src="jqueryui/js/jquery-ui-1.8.x.custom.min.js"
         type="text/javascript"></script>
        <script src="index.js" type="text/javascript"></script>

    </head>
```

```
<body style="font-size: 10px;">

    <div class="ui-widget ui-widget-content ui-state-default
      ui-corner-top" style="width: 25%;">

        <p style="text-align: center;">My Top Rounded
          Corners</p>

    </div>

</body>

</html>
```

2. Reload `index.html` in your web browser. You should see something similar to the following:

My Top Rounded Corners

What just happened?

We've modified the `div` element created in the previous example so that only the top left and right corners are round. The bottom left and right borders are straight. The only change we made to accomplish this is change the `ui-corner-all` class to `ui-corner-top`. This class will only apply corner roundness to the top left and top right corners of the element.

The `ui-corner-top` class does this by using both the `border-top-left-radius` and `border-top-right-radius` style properties. This is handy - we don't need to specify that we want to apply roundness to the top left and top right. Instead, we can apply the "corner top" abstraction created by the CSS framework.

Have a go hero

Try modifying the preceding example using the `ui-corner-bottom` class to set the bottom corners.

Time for action - setting individual corners

We've seen how to apply rounded corners to the entire element or to just one side of the element using the framework CSS classes. But what if I just want to set individual borders using a configuration not provided by the corner CSS abstractions?

1. Edit the `index.html` file created earlier and replace the content with the following:

```
<html xmlns="http://www.w3.org/1999/xhtml">

    <head>

        <title>Special Effects</title>

        <link href="jqueryui/development-bundle/themes/base/
          jquery.ui.all.css" rel="stylesheet" type="text/css" />

        <script src="jqueryui/js/jquery-1.5.x.min.js" type="text/
          javascript"></script>
        <script src="jqueryui/js/jquery-ui-1.8.x.custom.min.js"
          type="text/javascript"></script>
        <script src="index.js" type="text/javascript"></script>

    </head>

    <body style="font-size: 10px;">

        <div class="ui-widget ui-widget-content ui-state-default
          ui-corner-tl ui-corner-br" style="width: 25%;">

            <p style="text-align: center;">My Random Rounded
              Corners</p>

        </div>

    </body>

</html>
```

2. Reload `index.html` in your web browser. You should see something similar to the following:

What just happened?

We've just used the `ui-corner-tl` and `ui-corner-br` CSS classes to apply rounded corners to the top left and bottom right of our `div` element. This time, we had to use two classes instead of just one to accomplish what we wanted. Again, the classes take care of the browser compatibility issues.

Time for action - increasing corner roundness

So far, we've applied the default corner roundness to elements using the corner classes from the CSS framework. That is, themes come with a default corner radius value. If we build our theme using the ThemeRoller application, we can set this value here and get a preview of what our corners will look like applied to widgets. However, let's say we want to tweak the roundness of our corners without rebuilding the entire theme in ThemeRoller. We can make simple adjustments directly in the theme CSS.

1. Edit the `index.html` file created earlier and replace the content with the following:

```html
<html xmlns="http://www.w3.org/1999/xhtml">

    <head>

        <title>Special Effects</title>

        <link href="jqueryui/development-bundle/themes/base/
            jquery.ui.all.css" rel="stylesheet" type="text/css" />

        <script src="jqueryui/js/jquery-1.5.x.min.js" type="text/
            javascript"></script>
        <script src="jqueryui/js/jquery-ui-1.8.x.custom.min.js"
            type="text/javascript"></script>
        <script src="index.js" type="text/javascript"></script>

    </head>

    <body style="font-size: 10px;">

        <div class="ui-widget ui-widget-content ui-state-default
            ui-corner-all" style="width: 25%;">

            <p style="text-align: center;">My Rounded Corners</p>

        </div>

    </body>

</html>
```

2. In the `jqueryui/development-bundle/themes/base` **directory**, edit the `jquery.ui.theme.css` **file**.

3. Locate the `.ui-corner-all` style definition and replace it with the following:

```
.ui-corner-all {

    -moz-border-radius: 8px;
    -webkit-border-radius: 8px;
    border-radius: 8px;

}
```

4. Reload `index.html` in your web browser. You should see something similar to the following:

My Rounded Corners

What just happened?

In `index.html`, we have a simple `div` element with the `ui-corner-all` class applied to it. This class means that rounded corners will be applied to all corners of the element.

In `jquery.ui.theme.css`, we've updated the `.ui-corner-all` style definition to use a corner radius of 8px instead of 4px. This doubles the corner roundness - larger radius values mean a rounder corner. There are three properties we changed within this style - `-moz-border-radius`, `-webkit-border-radius`, and `border-radius`. This style encapsulates applying the border radius to different browsers with different levels of CSS compliance.

 If the browser finds a property it supports, the others are simply ignored. For example, with Firefox 4, the `border-radius` property is recognized, so if the `-moz-border-radius` property is encountered first, it will be dropped in favor of the `border-radius` property.

You'll notice that in `jquery.ui.theme.css`, we only changed one style definition - `ui-corner-all`. We did this because the elements in our example use rounded corners for all four corners. That is, the `div` element only applies to the `ui-corner-all` class. In a realistic application, more elaborate combinations will be used; some elements will have all corners rounded while others might only have the two top corners rounded. This is the drawback in using this approach - when we directly modify the CSS, we need to modify the border radius value for nine classes. In contrast, using the ThemeRoller application, we enter the value once and regenerate the theme CSS.

Having said that, there some scenarios where the ThemeRoller doesn't provide the flexibility we need in defining corners.

Experiment with different values for the border-radius property. For example, try increasing it or try using a different unit such as em.

Time for action - complex radius values

The values we've seen thus far for the border radius have used a single integer value. The border radius supports two values - a length from the side and a length from the top. When we supply a single value to this property, it is used for both lengths. If we want to use different values for these lengths, we'll need to customize the theme CSS:

1. Edit the index.html file created earlier and replace the content with the following:

```
<html xmlns="http://www.w3.org/1999/xhtml">

    <head>

        <title>Special Effects</title>

        <link href="jqueryui/development-bundle/themes/base/
          jquery.ui.all.css" rel="stylesheet" type="text/css" />

        <script src="jqueryui/js/jquery-1.5.x.min.js" type="text/
          javascript"></script>
        <script src="jqueryui/js/jquery-ui-1.8.x.custom.min.js"
          type="text/javascript"></script>
        <script src="index.js" type="text/javascript"></script>

    </head>

    <body style="font-size: 10px;">

        <div class="ui-widget ui-widget-content ui-state-default
          ui-corner-top" style="width: 25%;">

            <p style="text-align: center;">My Top Corners</p>

        </div>

    </body>

</html>
```

2. In the jqueryui/development-bundle/themes/base **directory, edit the** jquery.ui.theme.css **file.**

3. Locate the `.ui-corner-top` style definition and replace it with the following:

```
.ui-corner-top {

    -moz-border-radius-topleft: 10px 5px;
    -webkit-border-top-left-radius: 10px 5px;
    border-top-left-radius: 10px 5px;
    -moz-border-radius-topright: 10px 5px;
    -webkit-border-top-right-radius: 10px 5px;
    border-top-right-radius: 10px 5px;

}
```

4. Reload `index.html` in your web browser. You should see something similar to the following:

What just happened?

In `index.html`, we have a simple `div` element containing some text. This element has the `ui-corner-top` class applied to it. This makes the two top corners of the element rounded corners.

In `jquery.ui.theme.css`, we've updated the `ui-corner-top` class to use a complex border radius property. Instead of a single value, we now use two values. The first value, `10px`, gives the border radius from the side of the element. The second value, `5px`, gives the border radius from the top of the element. The resulting corner looks more like an arc, favoring the top of the element than a circle with the same curvature on both the top and side.

The same restrictions apply here as with the previous example. We've only modified the `ui-corner-top` class. This means that if we intend on having the same complex border radius affect all corners in our application, we'd need to be sure to update all corner classes with these values. But that may not be the case - maybe you only want this corner configuration applied to elements to top-corner roundness.

Time for action - using percentages

Another limitation of the ThemeRoller application with regard to the `border-radius` that determines the roundness of borders is that we're stuck using pixel values. This is fine in most circumstances. However, you might want to use a percentage value to determine the roundness of your element's corners:

_1._ Edit the `index.html` file created earlier and replace the content with the following:

```
<html xmlns="http://www.w3.org/1999/xhtml">

    <head>

        <title>Special Effects</title>

        <link href="jqueryui/development-bundle/themes/base/
          jquery.ui.all.css" rel="stylesheet" type="text/css" />

        <script src="jqueryui/js/jquery-1.5.x.min.js" type="text/
          javascript"></script>
        <script src="jqueryui/js/jquery-ui-1.8.x.custom.min.js"
          type="text/javascript"></script>
        <script src="index.js" type="text/javascript"></script>

    </head>

    <body style="font-size: 10px;">

        <div class="ui-widget ui-widget-content ui-state-default
          ui-corner-all" style="width: 20%; margin-bottom: 5px;">

            <p style="text-align: center;">Smaller Corners</p>

        </div>


        <div class="ui-widget ui-widget-content ui-state-default
          ui-corner-all" style="width: 400px; height: 40px;">

            <p style="text-align: center;">Larger Corners</p>

        </div>

    </body>

</html>
```

2. In the `jqueryui/development-bundle/themes/base` **directory, edit** `jquery.ui.theme.css`.

3. Locate the `.ui-corner-all` style definition and replace it with the following:

```
ui-corner-all {

    -moz-border-radius: 5%;
    -webkit-border-radius: 5%;
    border-radius: 5%;

}
```

4. Reload `index.html` in your web browser. You should see something similar to the following:

What just happened?

In `index.html`, we have two simple `div` elements. The first `div` is slightly smaller than the second `div`. Both elements have the `ui-corner-all` class applied to them.

In `jquery.ui.theme.css`, we've updated the property values of the `ui-corner-all` class to use percentage values instead of pixel values. This means that the `border-radius` is based on the size of the element and will change accordingly as the element size increases. We've illustrated this idea here with the two `div` elements. You'll notice that the corners of the larger `div` are slightly rounder than those of the smaller `div`. If we were to increase the size of either `div`, the roundness of the corners will also increase.

You'll want to exercise caution when using percentage values to define the roundness of theme corners. Although handy, they can sometimes lead to user interfaces looking disproportionate, the problem we're trying to solve with percentages in the first place. If you have many different widgets, all of varying sizes, chances are the percentage approach will not work out well because the corner roundness between widgets will be too different. On the other hand, lots of widgets that are similar in size can benefit from using percentages. The best advice here is to try using percentages first - you'll discover quickly whether they work for your theme or not. Fixed size pixel vales are always a good safeguard.

Time for action - removing corners

Rounded corners are a great feature of themes. They're aesthetically pleasing and easy to use. In fact, all jQuery UI widgets use rounded corners in one way or another. But what if you don't want rounded corners applied to your widget? There may be a case you need to adapt your theme to use a non-rounded version of a widget. Let's take a look at how this is done:

1. Edit the index.html file created earlier and replace the content with the following:

```html
<html xmlns="http://www.w3.org/1999/xhtml">

    <head>

        <title>Special Effects</title>

        <link href="jqueryui/development-bundle/themes/base/
          jquery.ui.all.css" rel="stylesheet" type="text/css" />

        <script src="jqueryui/js/jquery-1.5.x.min.js" type="text/
          javascript"></script>
        <script src="jqueryui/js/jquery-ui-1.8.x.custom.min.js"
          type="text/javascript"></script>
        <script src="index.js" type="text/javascript"></script>

    </head>

    <body style="font-size: 10px;">

        <div id="round_accordion" style="margin-bottom: 10px;
          width:25%;">

            <h3><a href="#">First</a></h3>
            <div>
                <p>First paragraph</p>
                <p>Second paragraph</p>
                <p>Third paragraph</p>
            </div>

            <h3><a href="#">Second</a></h3>
            <div></div>

            <h3><a href="#">Third</a></h3>
            <div></div>

        </div>
```

```
<div id="square_accordion" style="width: 25%;">

    <h3><a href="#">First</a></h3>
    <div>
        <p>First paragraph</p>
        <p>Second paragraph</p>
        <p>Third paragraph</p>
    </div>

    <h3><a href="#">Second</a></h3>
    <div></div>

    <h3><a href="#">Third</a></h3>
    <div></div>

</div>

</body>

</html>
```

2. Edit the `index.js` file created earlier and replace the content with the following:

```
$(document).ready(function(){

    $("#round_accordion").accordion();
    $("#square_accordion").accordion();

    $('#square_accordion .ui-corner-top').removeClass('ui-corner-
top');
    $('#square_accordion .ui-corner-bottom').removeClass('ui-
corner-bottom');
    $('#square_accordion .ui-corner-all').removeClass('ui-corner-
all');

});
```

3. Reload index.html in your web browser. You should see something similar to the following:

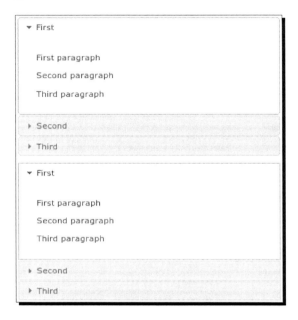

What just happened?

In index.html, we've created the markup for two accordion widgets. These two accordions are essential copies of each other. In index.js, we create the two accordion widgets once the page has finished loading - round_accordion and square_accordion. Next, as by default the widget uses round corners, we make the square_accordion use straight corners. This is done by removing the rounded corner classes from the widget's components. We don't even need to know ahead of time what these components are - we just need to check if they're applying a corner class. In this case, we've removed the ui-corner-top, ui-corner-bottom, and ui-corner-all classes from the accordion widget to make it square in appearance.

You're probably wondering why we removed corner classes from the widget instead of updating the class CSS. Aren't corners parts of the theme? Well, they are. However, what we've done here is remove a feature of the theme for a specific widget. We've said that "this accordion isn't going to apply any corner settings from the theme. This is a perfectly acceptable approach - to remove theme classes from where they don't apply. This is easy to do with jQuery UI themes as everything is encapsulated inside a class. This is an example of how we can adapt theme-friendly widgets to specific user interfaces (accordions look better without round corners). The preceding approach should be used sparingly - you shouldn't be removing classes from widget components frequently. Certainly not if the theme were called "squares".

Theme shadows

The jQuery UI theme framework has a class that, when applied, will give an element a shadow. This is an embellishment that may or may not be useful, depending on the application your theme is used with. For instance, users of mission-critical, enterprise software probably wouldn't appreciate shadows the same way as users of a website that talks about user interfaces.

There a number of properties in the `ui-widget-shadow` class, some of which overlap with what we've already seen in other classes. For instance, this class defines a background color and texture. It also uses rounded corners. In this section, we'll take a look at the different properties used in the `ui-widget-shadow` class definition. We'll also tweak these settings and apply theme to page elements.

Time for action - applying shadows

We're now going to take a look at how shadows are applied to jQuery UI widgets using the `ui-widget-shadow` class:

1. Edit the `index.html` file created earlier and replace the content with the following:

```
<html xmlns="http://www.w3.org/1999/xhtml">

    <head>

        <title>Special Effects</title>

        <link href="jqueryui/development-bundle/themes/base/
          jquery.ui.all.css" rel="stylesheet" type="text/css" />

        <script src="jqueryui/js/jquery-1.5.x.min.js" type="text/
          javascript"></script>
        <script src="jqueryui/js/jquery-ui-1.8.x.custom.min.js"
          type="text/javascript"></script>
        <script src="index.js" type="text/javascript"></script>

    </head>

    <body style="font-size: 10px;">

        <div style="margin: 20px;">

            <button id="my_button">My Button</button>

        </div>

    </body>

</html>
```

2. Edit the `index.js` file created earlier and replace the content with the following:

```
$(document).ready(function(){

    var btn, shadow;

    btn = $("#my_button").button();

    shadow = $("<div/>");

    shadow.width(btn.width());
    shadow.height(btn.height());
    shadow.addClass('ui-widget-shadow');

    shadow.css("position", "absolute");
    shadow.css("top", btn.position().top + 1);
    shadow.css("left", btn.position().left + 1);

    btn.parent().prepend(shadow);

});
```

3. Reload `index.html` in your web browser. You should see something similar to the following:

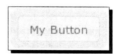

What just happened?

In `index.html`, we've created the markup for a simple jQuery UI button widget. The `button` element used for the widget is contained within a `div` element. This parent `div` element just gives the button element some space on the page.

In `index.js`, we create the button jQuery UI widget. Next, we create the `div` element that will apply the shadow to the button. We set the width and height of the shadow `div` to be the same as the width and height of the button. We then apply the `ui-widget-shadow` class. Next, we set some CSS properties on the `div` element to move it to the same location as the `button` element. Finally, we append the new `div` element to the button's container.

This example involves a lot of work on our part. We need to create a new element and adjust its position dynamically just so we can apply a `shadow` class? The good news is that jQuery provides us with the utilities to query computed dimensions and positions of DOM elements. We can then use these values to move the shadow behind our button element. So the code we've written can be adapted in other scenarios other than the one presented here. Once the `ui-widget-shadow` class is integrated into the button widget, we'll just need to set an option when creating the button. Until then, we'll have to live with writing additional eight or nine lines of code.

You can see the resulting button widget has something resembling a shadow surrounding it. So how does it work? In `index.js`, we created and configured the `div` that will apply the shadow. Recall that this `div` is in the same location and is exactly the same size as the button. So without the `ui-widget-shadow` class, we'd have just a regular button. The properties of the `ui-widget-shadow` class are what give the button its surrounding shadow. We'll explore these next.

Time for action - altering shadows

In the previous example, we created a button widget and applied a shadow to it using the `ui-widget-shadow` class. It is now time to take a closer look at the properties of this class and see what changes we can make to change the appearance of our theme shadows:

1. Reuse the same `index.html` and `index.js` files from the previous example. This will create a button widget and apply a shadow to it.

2. In the `jqueryui/development-bundle/themes/base` directory, edit the `jquery.ui.theme.css` file.

3. Locate the `.ui-widget-shadow` style definition and replace it with the following:

```css
.ui-widget-shadow {

    margin: -4px 0 0 -4px;
    padding: 4px;
    background: #aaaaaa url(images/ui-bg_flat_0_aaaaaa_40x100.png)
50% 50% repeat-x;
    opacity: .12;
    filter:Alpha(Opacity=12);
    -moz-border-radius: 4px;
    -webkit-border-radius: 4px;
    border-radius: 4px;

}
```

4. Reload `index.html` in your web browser. You should see something similar to the following:

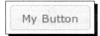

What just happened?

We've reused the same button widget and applied the same shadow from the previous example. In `jquery.ui.theme.css`, we've made a number of changes to the `ui-widget-shadow` class that makes it much subtler than the previous version. We changed the thickness of the shadow. This was accomplished by changing the padding value from `8px` to `4px`. To compensate for this change, we also had to adjust the margin value by replacing `8px` with `4px`. We'll see why this is important later.

◆ We changed the opacity of the shadow from `30%` to `12%`. This is quite the adjustment, but the end result is something that looks more like a shadow than a border. To do this we had to update the opacity and filter properties. It is worth noting that the filter property only applies to Internet Explorer.

◆ We changed the roundness of the shadow borders. The border radius went from `8px` to `4px`.

The misleading property of this class is the margin. We had to compensate for changes made to the shadow thickness here. But why is that? As we'll see next, the margin property controls the shadow offset relative to the element to which it is applied.

Time for action - changing perspectives

The shadows we've seen so far look like they're originating from the front of the widget - like the user is pointing a flashlight directly at it. But what if we move that flashlight up and to the left?

1. Reuse the same `index.html` and `index.js` files from the previous example. This will create a button widget and apply a shadow to it.

2. In the `jqueryui/development-bundle/themes/base` directory, edit `jquery.ui.theme.css`.

3. Locate the `.ui-widget-shadow` style definition and replace it with the following:

```
.ui-widget-shadow {

    margin: 2px 0 0 2px;
    padding: 2px;
```

```
    background: #aaaaaa url(images/ui-bg_flat_0_aaaaaa_40x100.png)
50% 50% repeat-x;
    opacity: .12;
    filter: Alpha(Opacity=12);
    -moz-border-radius: 4px;
    -webkit-border-radius: 4px;
    border-radius: 4px;

}
```

4. Reload `index.html` in your web browser. You should see something similar to the following:

What just happened?

In `index.html`, we're using the same button widget and applying the same shadow as in the previous example.

In `jquery.ui.theme.css`, we've also used many of the same properties in the `ui-widget-shadow` class. What have changed, however, are the `margin` and the `padding` properties. We've altered them to make the shadows in our theme to appear as though they're originating from the top-left of the screen.

Remember, the div that applies the shadow is the same size as the button widget. The `margin` property in the `ui-widget-shadow` class is what makes the shadow visible outside the boundaries of the widget. For instance, the negative top and left margin values in the previous example mean that the shadow is displayed outside of the button. Here, we've changed these to values to positive integers which is what pushes the shadow down and to the right. We've also compensated for this change by lessening the shadow depth. This is controlled by the `padding` property.

Theme overlays

The jQuery UI theme framework provides a CSS class for overlaying other widgets in your user interface. The most common use for this class is to call attention to something by overlaying all irrelevant page elements with a semi-transparent layer. For instance, you can use this class to call attention to a message box by applying the class to all other elements aside from the message itself. The jQuery UI dialog widget uses this class to overlay the entire UI except for the dialog when it is displayed.

We have the ability to change the appearance of overlays used in our theme. The dialog is by far the most common use of this class, although, it could be used to overlay individual elements rather than the entire screen.

Time for action - adjusting dialog overlays

It's time to make some changes to the `ui-widget-overlay` class and see how they look when a dialog widget is displayed:

1. Edit the `index.html` file created earlier and replace the content with the following:

```
<html xmlns="http://www.w3.org/1999/xhtml">

    <head>

        <title>Special Effects</title>

        <link href="jqueryui/development-bundle/themes/base/
         jquery.ui.all.css" rel="stylesheet" type="text/css" />

        <script src="jqueryui/js/jquery-1.5.x.min.js" type="text/
         javascript"></script>
        <script src="jqueryui/js/jquery-ui-1.8.x.custom.min.js"
         type="text/javascript"></script>
        <script src="index.js" type="text/javascript"></script>

    </head>

    <body style="font-size: 10px;">

        <div id="my_dialog">

            <p>Some dialog content</p>

        </div>

    </body>

</html>
```

2. Edit the `index.js` file created earlier and replace the content with the following:

```
$(document).ready(function(){

    $("#my_dialog").dialog({title: "My Dialog", modal: true});

});
```

3. In the `jqueryui/development-bundle/themes/base` directory, edit the `jquery.ui.theme.css` file.

4. Locate the `.ui-widget-overlay` style definition and replace it with the following:

```
.ui-widget-overlay {

    background:  #aaaaaa;
    opacity:  .2;
    filter:Alpha(Opacity=20);

}
```

5. Reload `index.html` in your web browser. You should see something similar to the following:

What just happened?

We've just altered the overlay that covers the user interface when the dialog widget is displayed. In `index.html`, we have a simple `div` element that is tuned into a jQuery UI dialog widget in `index.js` when the page has finished loading.

In `jquery.ui.theme.css`, we've removed the background image from the `ui-widget-overlay` class as the dialog over has no texture. Widget texture is defined by background images and as the `ui-widget-overlay` class is using a flat color, the texture image is redundant. Consequently, the user interface will no longer need to load this image. We've also lessened the opacity of the dialog. This way, widgets are slightly more visible when the dialog is displayed, yet it remains obvious that they're still disabled until that dialog is closed.

Summary

In this chapter, we've seen what the jQuery UI theme framework has to offer for special effects. This includes rounded corners, shadows, and overlays. These effects are strictly theme effects, not jQuery UI effects. The toolkit does provide fancy animation effects used when transitioning between two element states. However, these have nothing to do with themes and are outside the scope of this book.

The theme framework gives us an array of classes we can use to change the roundness of corners. This is a step away from the legacy approach of superimposing images to give the appearance of roundness. Depending on where we want to apply the round corner, the top, the bottom, or the entire element, we have a class that will do it. The corner classes of the framework use a `border-radius` to determine the roundness. We've seen several variations of manipulating and applying borders in this chapter.

The shadow special effect gives elements to which it is applied a three-dimensional appearance. This class is not quite as developed as the corner classes and it takes a little more work to apply it correctly. We can alter this class in our themes to change the thickness, as well as the perspective of the shadow.

The overlay effect calls attention to widgets such as dialogs by adding a semi-transparent layer of the rest of the user interface. This is a useful effect, utilized by the dialog widget. We can change the style properties of this class to change the way the dialog looks.

Now that we've explored the vast majority of the `jquery.ui.theme.css` file, it's time to take a closer look at what all these other theme CSS files do. These are for built-in widgets provided by jQuery UI. In the next chapter, we'll see what is involved when we're building our own widgets.

9

Theming Custom Widgets

Themes aren't limited to the widgets that ship with jQuery UI. You'll often find yourself wanting to create your own widgets that fit a particular use case. These new widgets have to look like they fit in the theme otherwise they'll look out of place.

In this chapter we shall:

◆ Create a custom widget

◆ Make our custom widget theme-ready

◆ Look at reusing core widget themes

So let's get on with it.

What are custom widgets?

The jQuery UI JavaScript toolkit comes with several widgets. The goal of this book is to understand the CSS theme framework that comes with jQuery UI. To fully understand the theme framework, we need a working knowledge of the widget framework. This is because we're eventually going to be creating themes for custom widgets.

A custom widget is really no different from a built-in widget, aside from the fact that they don't ship with jQuery UI—and that really is the big difference. You can think of widgets that ship with jQuery UI as several custom widgets. The jQuery UI core is the common facility that unites the built-in widgets and custom widgets created by others.

The jQuery UI library defines an abstract widget called **Widget**. This is never created by a user interface. Instead, all jQuery UI widgets inherit from Widget. This is how the jQuery plugin component is created. The plugin is why we're able to say things such as "turn this button element into a button widget". In addition to inheriting from Widget, custom widgets can also extend built-in widgets. We can even extend and build upon our own custom widgets.

Widget JS

What does a jQuery UI widget implementation look like? Widgets are implemented using JavaScript. A widget is instantiated like any other jQuery plugin—a method is called on a selector. These widget constructors need a selector because each matched element will eventually become the widget. For example, a button element on a page might eventually become a jQuery UI button widget. To make this transformation, we need to select the button element and call the button widget constructor on it. We can't, for example, call a button widget on a table element or with no selector at all. Widgets are dependent on DOM elements. This relationship is illustrated as follows:

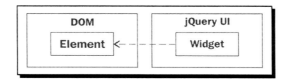

We can see here that widgets depend on elements in the DOM and not the other way around. Imagine building widgets that had no underlying DOM structure. If you were to remove jQuery UI from the equation, you'd have no user interface. The goal of jQuery UI widgets is to enhance the appearance of standard DOM elements using a consistent theme framework. There are some other features of widgets that we'll see throughout this chapter.

Widget CSS

Throughout the preceding chapters, we've seen several standard jQuery UI widgets in use—button, accordion, tabs. We've seen how these widgets change in appearance as we've updated our theme design. This is made possible by CSS classes from the framework. It is the responsibility of the widget to apply these classes to the element. In addition to applying general theme classes to the element, the widget must also apply classes from the theme specific to that widget. These classes use style properties that don't apply to other widgets. The relationship between widgets and their CSS modules is illustrated in the following diagram:

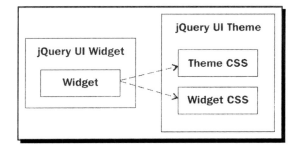

We can see here that any given widget that is part of the jQuery UI widget framework requires two CSS components. The theme framework must provide the general theme component, the part we've studied throughout this book, and a component specific to the widget.

So what exactly does the widget CSS do? The short answer is, it applies style properties specific to that widget. This is things like margins and padding. There some properties in the general theme CSS that are overridden by properties in the specific widget CSS. For example, a widget component that uses the `ui-widget-content` class might not want a border on the bottom. The widget CSS would override this property. This way, the remaining borders of the component still adhere to the general theme.

Widget CSS rarely changes between different jQuery UI themes. User interfaces use different themes mainly because they need a different look and feel. This is controlled by the general theme CSS and applied to all widgets. But different user interfaces might use different widgets. As we'll see in this chapter, we'll need a way to apply specific styles to our custom widgets. These styles become part of any themes we use in our user interface.

Pop quiz – jQuery UI widgets

1. What is the difference between the core jQuery UI widgets and custom jQuery UI widgets?

    a. The only difference between the core jQuery UI widgets and custom widgets is that the latter aren't included with jQuery UI. Otherwise, they're built the same way.

    b. Custom widgets don't require CSS whereas the core jQuery UI widgets do.

    c. Custom widgets depend on DOM elements whereas the core widgets do not.

2. What are the two types of CSS a widget must implement?

    a. Any jQuery UI widget needs classes from the CSS framework applied to it. The widget must also implement CSS styles specific to the widget such as padding and margins.

    b. Widgets only need to provide CSS specific to the widget.

    c. CSS is completely optional with widgets.

3. Why do widgets depend on DOM elements on an HTML page?

    a. Widgets depend on DOM elements because a key principle behind jQuery UI widgets is taking a plain HTML element and extending it with features and proving a consistent look and feel.

    b. Widgets don't depend on DOM elements.

    c. Widgets require DOM elements so they can respond to events triggered by the element.

Implementing widgets

For the remainder of the chapter, we're going to build our own widget and theme it. We first need to implement the widget before we apply styles to it. This section is mostly concerned with the HTML markup and JavaScript implementation of the widget. In the next section, we'll focus on styling our widget in a theme-friendly way.

The widget

We're going to design an inbox widget. The goal of this widget is to display a concise list of messages to the user. The widget would most likely serve as a front-end to an e-mail application. We're going to keep the widget generalized enough that it isn't bound specifically to act as an interface for an e-mail inbox. It might be used as a front-end for viewing text messages.

The requirements of this widget are fairly straightforward. It has to display a list of messages in a truncated form – only the subject, sender, and date. The user must be able to open a message and read it. Finally, it needs to differentiate between read and unread messages.

We'll need to keep in mind that this is simply a widget, not a user interface. There is a lot that our widget doesn't do – the widget doesn't actually send or receive any messages. It doesn't perform any kind of validation. Recall that widgets are much more useful if they're not bound to a particular application domain. We'll see, however, that we can design our widgets with implementing them in mind by providing entry points that allow applications to use it.

Time for action – basic markup

It's now time to see how our widget looks as basic HTML markup. This will serve as the basis for our widget layout design. As will all jQuery UI widgets, we need a strong HTML foundation to build upon. The HTML of our widget will also help us decide which elements are important for the widget theme:

1. If you haven't already, download and extract the jQuery UI package into a directory called jQuery UI from `http://jqueryui.com/download`.

2. At the same level as the jQuery UI directory, create a new `index.html` file with the following content:

```
<html xmlns="http://www.w3.org/1999/xhtml">

    <head>

        <title>Theming Custom Widgets</title>

    </head>

    <body style="font-size: 10px;">

        <div>

            <h1>Inbox</h1>

            <ul>

                <li>
                    <span>Joe - <i>Phone</i></span>
                    <a href="#">Open</a>
                    <div>Whats your phone # again?</div>

                </li>

                <li>
                    <span>Megan - <i>Hi</i></span>
                    <a href="#">Open</a>
                    <div>Hey!  Whats up?  I got a new laptop!</div>

                </li>

                <li>
                    <span>The Boss - <i>Late</i></span>
                    <a href="#">Open</a>
                    <div>Where are you?</div>
```

```
                                </li>

                            </ul>

                        </div>

                    </body>

                </html>
```

3. Reload `index.html` in your web browser. You should see something similar to the following:

What just happened?

We've just assembled the HTML markup that will serve as the structural basis for our widget. There aren't any styles applied to any of these elements. Thankfully, this is only temporary. We don't want the task of applying styles to obscure the structural backbone of the widget. There is a fair amount going on here even without any styles. So we'll walk through each piece.

Inside the body of our HTML document, we have a `div` element. This is where our inbox widget starts. Elements inside this `div` are the inbox components. Next, we have an `h1` header element that gives the inbox its name. Already, we see something that might be customized as not everyone will want this widget to be called inbox in their user interface. Following the header, we have a `ul` unordered list element. This is where our messages are stored.

Each `li` list item shown here represents an individual inbox message. We have three here to provide us with some example content. The first element inside each list item is a `span`. The `span` contains the name of the message sender and the message subject. The subject is italicized to differentiate it from the sender. Next, we have an open link. This is supposed to open the message, although it doesn't do anything at this point. Remember, we're still just creating the widget mock-up. Finally, we have the message content itself inside a `div`.

Goals of the widget

We've conveyed above what our inbox widget is supposed to do, so we already know its goals. Well, maybe not exactly. Armed with the widget HTML markup, we can identify some more specifics regarding how we might go about implementing such a widget. These things are nearly impossible to foresee until we have something to look at as we do now. Especially the visual design.

Looking at the output of our raw widget HTML, what we have is an eyesore. In its current state, the inbox widget has no business in a user interface of any kind. Obviously we need to add some styles to the widget. The eventual goal is to style our widget using classes from the jQuery UI framework. So what are some of the visual improvements we want to make?

The widget as a whole should probably be self-contained somehow, perhaps using a border and a background of one sort or another. Otherwise, the inbox looks like it's randomly placed on the page. The list items – the listed messages of the inbox, could probably use better isolation from one another. In their current form, each list item is difficult to tell apart from one another because they're so close together.

The message content is displayed just below the message sender and subject. We've only used short messages here as example content. Obviously this wont do for longer messages. So we should probably hide the message body entirely until its opened for reading.

These are just the more obvious improvements we'd want to make visually. There are likely to be more once we start implementing it. At this point, we can also start thinking about the functional aspects of the widget. What options and methods will it support? We'll touch on these a bit later but the main focus here is on extending the jQuery UI theme to support our widget.

Time for action – basic JavaScript

It's time to write the initial JavaScript code that will provide the jQuery plugin for turning regular HTML elements into widgets:

1. Edit the `index.html` file created earlier and replace the content with the following:

```
<html xmlns="http://www.w3.org/1999/xhtml">

    <head>

        <title>Theming Custom Widgets</title>

        <link href="jqueryui/development-bundle/themes/base/
jquery.ui.all.css" rel="stylesheet" type="text/css" />
```

```
        <script src="jqueryui/js/jquery-1.5.x.min.js" type="text/
javascript"></script>
        <script src="jqueryui/js/jquery-ui-1.8.x.custom.min.js"
type="text/javascript"></script>
        <script src="jquery.ui.inbox.js" type="text/javascript"></
script>
        <script src="index.js" type="text/javascript"></script>

    </head>

    <body style="font-size: 10px;">

        <div id="inbox">

            <h1>Inbox</h1>

            <ul>

                <li>
                    <span>Joe - <i>Phone</i></span>
                    <a href="#">Open</a>
                    <div>Whats your phone # again?</div>

                </li>

                <li>
                    <span>Megan - <i>Hi</i></span>
                    <a href="#">Open</a>
                    <div>Hey!  Whats up?  I got a new laptop!</
div>

                </li>

                <li>
                    <span>The Boss - <i>Late</i></span>
                    <a href="#">Open</a>
                    <div>Where are you?</div>

                </li>

            </ul>

        </div>

    </body>

</html>
```

2. In the same directory as `index.html`, create a new file called index.js and add the following content:

```
$(document).ready(function(){

    $('#inbox').inbox({title: 'My Inbox'});

});
```

3. In the same directory as `index.html`, create a new file called `jquery.ui.inbox.js` and add the following content:

```
$.widget('ui.inbox', {

    options: {

        title: null

    },

    _init: function () {

        var title = this.options.title;

        if (title !== null) {

            this.element
                .children('h1:first-child')
                .html(title);

        }

    }

});
```

4. Reload `index.html` in your web browser. You should see something similar to the following:

My Inbox

- Joe - *Phone* Open
  Whats your phone # again?
- Megan - *Hi* Open
  Hey! Whats up? I got a new laptop!
- The Boss - *Late* Open
  Where are you?

What just happened?

We've just implemented our first jQuery UI widget! Well, it's not much of a widget just yet, but we've taken care of the boilerplate stuff that doesn't change much if at all. Let's walk through what we've just done before we start making more drastic visual changes to our widget.

In `index.html`, we've included the jQuery UI theme stylesheet along with several Javascript files. The first two – jQuery core and jQuery UI – are required in order for any jQuery UI widgets to work. The next JavaScript file, `jquery.ui.inbox.js`, is our widget module. Finally, the `index.js` file contains JavaScript that runs when the page has finished loading. We've also added an id attribute to our widget div element so we may reference it later on.

In `index.js`, we've added an event callback function that triggers when the page has finished loading as we've seen throughout all the preceding chapters. This callback finds our inbox `div` element and calls the inbox widget constructor on it.

In `jquery.ui.inbox.js`, we define the inbox widget. We've kept the jQuery UI module naming convention with `jquery.ui.inbox.js`. This is clearly a module that defines a widget.

 Widgets are defined using the `$.widget` factory. Calling this actually creates the widget by adding to the ui plugin name space.

You can see we're using the ui name space by specifying the widget name as 'ui.inbox'. This is the first argument to the widget factory. The second argument is an object that defines the attributes and methods of the widget.

The first attribute we have is called `options` and is treated specially by jQuery UI. The `options` attribute specifies default values for the widget constructor. Here, we're providing a default `title`. In `index.js`, we've changed the default title to `My Inbox` when we created the widget. The `_init` method is also treated specially by jQuery UI. This is called for us automatically when the widget is created. In the `_init` method, `this.element` refers to the `div` we called the inbox constructor on. This is stored as an attribute by jQuery automatically so the widget can manipulate the HTML element.

In `index.js`, we've added one small feature to the widget already – setting the title. The `title` option of the inbox is used in the `_init` method to replace the current title if specified. We do this by locating the `h1` element and replacing its HTML with the new title. If the title option wasn't specified, the existing title is used.

Time for action – adding more behavior

Now that we've set up the Javascript foundation for our widget, we're ready to add some more behavior to it before we start adding styles:

1. Edit the jquery.ui.inbox.js file created earlier and replace the content with the following:

```
$.widget('ui.inbox', {

    options: {

        title: null

    },

    _init: function () {

        var title = this.options.title;

        if (title !== null) {

            this.element
                .children('h1:first-child')
                .html(title);

        }

        this.element
            .find('ul li div')
            .hide();

        this.element
            .append($('<div></div>')
            .addClass('inbox-dlg'));

        this.element
            .children('div.inbox-dlg')
            .dialog({autoOpen: false});

        this.element
            .find('ul li a')
            .button()
            .click(function(){
```

```
                    $(this).blur()
                            .parent()
                            .addClass('inbox-read');

                    var subject = $(this).siblings('span').html();
                    var body = $(this).siblings('div').html();

                    $('div.inbox-dlg').html(body)
                                        .dialog('option', {title:
        subject})
                                        .dialog('open');

                });

            }

        });
```

2. Reload `index.html` in your web browser and click **Open** on one of the messages. You should see something similar to the following:

What just happened?

We've just added some more behavioral features to our inbox widget Javascript. Most of these changes are in the widget constructor. We're also using two built-in widgets – the button and the dialog. Often, when building custom jQuery UI widgets, it makes sense to reuse these pre-built components. Let's walk through the changes we've made.

Each message in our inbox is a list item – a `li` element. Inside each list item we have the message sender, subject, and body. Now, we don't want to display the body because this can be rather large. So in the inbox constructor, we hide the body `div` element with the following:

```
this.element
    .find('ul li div')
    .hide();
```

Next, we create the `div` element that will serve as the message dialog. Now that we hide the message body when the instance is created, we need a way to display it. We give the div an `inbox-dlg` class so we can reference it after it has been added to the widget DOM. Next, we call the dialog constructor. Here we tell the dialog to not open automatically:

```
this.element
    .append($('<div></div>')
    .addClass('inbox-dlg'));

this.element
    .children('div.inbox-dlg')
    .dialog({autoOpen: false});
```

Lastly, we find all the links in our widget that open messages. We need to do two things with the open links. First, we need to turn them into button widgets. This is done with the following code:

```
this.element
    .find('ul li a')
    .button()
```

This turns the set of matched link elements into jQuery UI buttons. In this same matched set, we attach a `click` event function. This is called when the user clicks the open button. The first thing we want to do is blur the focus of the button when clicked. Otherwise, we'll see some strange behavior after the displayed dialog is closed. Then we want to add a class to the containing list item – `inbox-read`. This class indicates that the message has been read:

```
$(this).blur()
    .parent()
    .addClass('inbox-read');
```

The final job of our `click` callback is to actually display the dialog with the subject and message. First, we need to extract the subject and body to display in the dialog. This is done by calling the `html()` method on the `span` and `div` elements contained in the message list item:

```
var subject = $(this).siblings('span').html();
var body = $(this).siblings('div').html();
```

Now we can display the dialog using these values. First we set the dialog content and title, and then we open it:

```
$('div.inbox-dlg').html(body)
                             .dialog('option', {title:
subject})
                             .dialog('open');
```

We now have a fully-functional widget that does almost everything we want it to do. It still needs a lot of styling work, however, before it is ready for prime time.

Styling widgets

The style of any jQuery UI widget has two parts – the widget style and the theme style. The widget style will handle things like basic layout of the widget's components. The theme style applies classes from the theme CSS framework. The appearance of the widget is based on the current theme. Without applying these theme classes, our widget will not be theme-friendly. However, our widget CSS might override some style rules set by the theme CSS. This section explores how we use the two levels of CSS definitions to control the look and feel of our custom jQuery UI widgets.

Time for action – widget CSS

It's time for us to improve the visual appearance of our widget. We'll start by creating some widget-specific styles:

1. Edit the `index.html` file created earlier and replace the content with the following:

```
<html xmlns="http://www.w3.org/1999/xhtml">

    <head>

        <title>Theming Custom Widgets</title>

        <link href="jqueryui/development-bundle/themes/base/
jquery.ui.all.css" rel="stylesheet" type="text/css" />
        <link href="jquery.ui.inbox.css" rel="stylesheet"
type="text/css" />

        <script src="jqueryui/js/jquery-1.5.x.min.js" type="text/
javascript"></script>
        <script src="jqueryui/js/jquery-ui-1.8.x.custom.min.js"
type="text/javascript"></script>
        <script src="jquery.ui.inbox.js" type="text/javascript"></
script>
```

```
            <script src="index.js" type="text/javascript"></script>

    </head>

    <body style="font-size: 10px;">

        <div style="width: 30%;">

            <div id="inbox">

                <h1>Inbox</h1>

                <ul>

                    <li>
                        <span>Joe - <i>Phone</i></span>
                        <a href="#">Open</a>
                        <div>Whats your phone # again?</div>

                    </li>

                    <li>
                        <span>Megan - <i>Hi</i></span>
                        <a href="#">Open</a>
                        <div>Hey!  Whats up?  I got a new
laptop!</div>

                    </li>

                    <li>
                        <span>The Boss - <i>Late</i></span>
                        <a href="#">Open</a>
                        <div>Where are you?</div>

                    </li>

                </ul>

            </div>

        </div>

    </body>

</html>
```

2. Edit the jquery.ui.inbox.js file created earlier and replace the content with the following:

```
$.widget('ui.inbox', {

    options: {

        title: null

    },

     _init: function () {

        var title = this.options.title,
            baseClasses = 'ui-inbox';

        this.element.addClass(baseClasses);

        if (title !== null) {

            this.element
                .children('h1:first-child')
                .html(title);

        }

        this.element
            .find('ul li div')
            .hide();

        this.element
            .find('ul li').append($('<div></div>')
            .addClass('ui-helper-clearfix'));

        this.element
            .append($('<div></div>')
            .addClass('inbox-dlg'));

        this.element
            .children('div.inbox-dlg')
            .dialog({autoOpen: false});

        this.element
            .find('ul li a')
```

```
                    .button()
                    .click(function(){

                         $(this).blur()
                                .parent()
                                .addClass('inbox-read');

                         var subject = $(this).siblings('span').html();
                         var body = $(this).siblings('div').html();

                         $('div.inbox-dlg').html(body)
                                          .dialog('option', {title:
subject})
                                          .dialog('open');

                    });

               }

          });
```

3. In the same directory as the `index.html` and `jquery.ui.inbox.js` files, create a new `jquery.ui.inbox.css` file with the following content:

```css
.ui-inbox {

     padding: 10px;
     width: 100%;

}

.ui-inbox ul {

     margin: 0px;
     padding: 0px;

}

.ui-inbox ul li {

     list-style-type: none;
     margin: 3px;

}
```

```
.ui-inbox ul li a {

    float: right;

}
```

4. Reload `index.html` in your web browser. You should see something similar to the following:

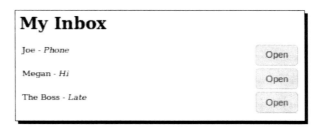

What just happened?

We've just implemented styles specific to our widget. In index.html, we've made a few minor changes. First, we've included the new stylesheet that defines our widget styles. Second, the `#inbox div` that defines the structure of our widget is now contained within another `div`. This container `div` specifies a width for our widget. We'll see why this is important momentarily.

 It is good practice to follow the same naming convention as the core jQuery UI widgets. Our example uses `jquery.ui.inbox.js` and `jquery.ui.inbox.css` for the widget JavaScript and widget CSS respectively. Keeping the file naming convention consistent with any custom widgets you create will make them easier to manage. Especially once you start implementing several widgets.

We've also made a few changes to our widget Javascript in jquery.ui.inbox.js. In the constructor, we've created a new `baseClasses` variable. This is used to name the base CSS classes applied to our widget. In this case, we've only added `ui-inbox`. We've used the name `baseClasses` because this is a jQuery UI idiom and we want to be consistent. We then apply the base CSS classes to the element with `this.element.addClass(baseClasses);`. We're also adding a new div to each list item as follows:

```
this.element
    .find('ul li').append($('<div></div>')
    .addClass('ui-helper-clearfix'));
```

Didn't we say we weren't going to add any classes from the theme framework yet? We did, and `ui-helper-clearfix` is one of many utility classes offered by the framework. These utilities are used by widgets for common tasks like clearing float alignment and aren't exactly theme specific. We'll see in a moment why this class is necessary.

In `jquery.ui.inbox.css`, we've defined the CSS styles specific to our inbox widget. The first style definition is `.ui-inbox`. This is the general class applied to the entire widget. This style gives the widget some padding and sets the width to `100%`. Recall in index.html, we moved the widget `div` into a container `div`. Setting the `width` property here will ensure that the widget uses the width defined by its parent. The padding property gives the inbox widget some space from surrounding elements as is illustrated below:

The next style definition is `.ui-inbox ul`. This style is used to remove the list indentation. Lists, by default, are indented by browsers. Setting the margin and padding to 0px will ensure our widget's list of messages aren't indented.

The next style affects individual list items and is defined as `.ui-inbox ul li`. Here, we use the `list-style-type` property to remove the bullets from the list. Again, this is another browser default that we can do without. This style also gives list items a margin that provides some space between them as illustrated below:

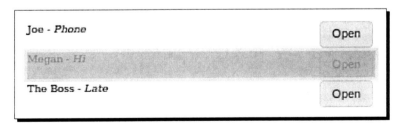

The final widget-specific style affects links and is defined as `.ui-inbox ul li a`. This style tells the open buttons to `float` to the `right` of each message list item. This gives the sender and subject some space.

Time for action – theme CSS

Now that we've implemented some widget-specific CSS, it's time to make our widget theme-friendly by applying some classes from the jQuery UI theme framework:

1. Edit the `jquery.ui.inbox.js` file created earlier and replace the content with the following:

```
$.widget('ui.inbox', {

    options: {

        title: null

    },

    _init: function () {

        var title = this.options.title,
            baseClasses = 'ui-inbox ui-widget ui-widget-content',
            headerClasses = 'ui-widget-header',
            messageClasses = 'ui-widget-content ui-state-default';

        this.element
            .addClass(baseClasses)
            .children('h1')
            .addClass(headerClasses);

        this.element
            .find('ul li')
            .addClass(messageClasses);

        if (title !== null) {

            this.element
                .children('h1:first-child')
                .html(title);

        }

        this.element
            .find('ul li div')
            .hide();

        this.element
            .find('ul li').append($('<div></div>')
            .addClass('ui-helper-clearfix'));
```

```
this.element
    .append($('<div></div>')
    .addClass('inbox-dlg'));

this.element
    .children('div.inbox-dlg')
    .dialog({autoOpen: false});

this.element
    .find('ul li a')
    .button()
    .click(function(){

        $(this).blur()
                .parent()
                .addClass('inbox-read');

        var subject = $(this).siblings('span').html();
        var body = $(this).siblings('div').html();

        $('div.inbox-dlg').html(body)
                            .dialog('option', {title:
subject})
                            .dialog('open');

    });

}

});
```

2. Reload `index.html` in your web browser. You should see something similar to the following:

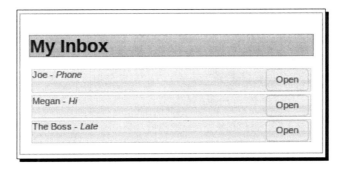

What just happened?

We've just updated our widget JavaScript to make it theme-friendly. In `jquery.ui.inbox.js`, we've updated the `baseClasses` variable and added two new variables to the inbox constructor as follows:

```
baseClasses = 'ui-inbox ui-widget ui-widget-content',
headerClasses = 'ui-widget-header',
messageClasses = 'ui-widget-content ui-state-default';
```

The `baseClasses` variable now has three classes – `ui-inbox`, `ui-widget`, and `ui-widget-content`. The latter two classes are from the theme framework. The `headerClasses` variable uses the `ui-widget-header` class. The `messageClasses` variable has the `ui-widget-content` and `ui-state-default` classes from the theme framework.

The `baseClasses` variable is already used to apply the stored classes to the widget. So the widget, as a whole, now has two new classes from the framework applied to it. This highlights the benefit of storing classes we apply to our widgets in variables – this change only involved us adding to the already-existing string.

The `headerClasses` variable is new so we had to add code in the widget constructor to apply it to the widget as follows:

```
this.element
    .addClass(baseClasses)
    .children('h1')
    .addClass(headerClasses);
```

We're simply building on the same statement that applies `baseClasses` here. The `messageClasses` variable is also new, so we need to apply it to each displayed list item in our widget. This is done as follows:

```
this.element
    .find('ul li')
    .addClass(messageClasses);
```

Time for action – finishing touches

At this point, our inbox widget is full-featured and theme-friendly. It does what it was designed to do and we can change themes. However, to make our widget as good as it can possibly be, we'll have to perform a final round of tweaks and enhancements:

1. Edit the `index.js` file created earlier and replace the content with the following:

```
$(document).ready(function(){

    $('#inbox').inbox({title: 'My Inbox',
```

```
                        icons: {'primary':'ui-icon-folder-open'}});

});
```

2 Edit the `jquery.ui.inbox.js` file created earlier and replace the content with the following:

```
$.widget('ui.inbox', {

    options: {

        title: null,
        icons: null,

    },

        _init: function () {

        var title = this.options.title,
            baseClasses = 'ui-inbox ui-widget ui-widget-content
ui-corner-all',
            headerClasses = 'ui-widget-header ui-corner-all',
            messageClasses = 'ui-widget-content ui-state-default
ui-state-highlight ui-corner-all';

        this.element
            .addClass(baseClasses)
            .children('h1')
            .addClass(headerClasses);

        this.element
            .find('ul li')
            .addClass(messageClasses);

        if (title !== null) {

            this.element
                .children('h1:first-child')
                .html(title);

        }

        this.element
            .find('ul li div')
            .hide();
```

```
this.element
    .find('ul li').append($('<div></div>')
    .addClass('ui-helper-clearfix'));

this.element
    .append($('<div></div>')
    .addClass('inbox-dlg'));

this.element
    .children('div.inbox-dlg')
    .dialog({autoOpen: false});

this.element
    .find('ul li a')
    .button({icons:this.options.icons})
    .click(function(){

        $(this).blur()
                .parent()
                .removeClass('ui-state-highlight');

        var subject = $(this).siblings('span').html();
        var body = $(this).siblings('div').html();

        $('div.inbox-dlg').html(body)
                            .dialog('option', {title:
subject})
                            .dialog('open');

    });

    }

});
```

3. Edit the `jquery.ui.inbox.css` file created earlier and replace the content with the following:

```
.ui-inbox {

    padding: 10px;
    width: 100%;

}

.ui-inbox h1 {

    margin-top: 0px;
    padding: 3px;
```

```
}

.ui-inbox ul {

    margin: 0px;
    padding: 0px;

}

.ui-inbox ul li {

    list-style-type: none;
    margin: 3px;
    padding: 3px;

}

.ui-inbox ul li a {

    float: right;

}

.ui-inbox ul li > span {

    position: absolute;
    margin-top: 0.5em;

}
```

4. Reload index.html in your web browser. You should see something similar to the following:

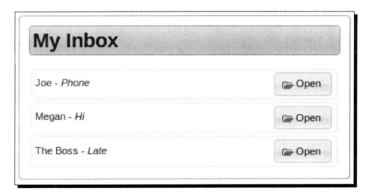

What just happened?

We've made several minor adjustments to our inbox widget that adds some finishing polish to it. We've added rounded corners, icons to the open button, and changed the way read messages are displayed. Let's walk through what we've changed exactly.

Most of the changes we've made are in jquery.ui.inbox.js – the Javascript module that defines our widget. To add rounded corners to our widget, we apply the `ui-corner-all` class to its components. We do this by extending our CSS class variables used in the constructor as follows, which will apply rounded corners to the entire widget, the widget header, and each list item:

```
            baseClasses = 'ui-inbox ui-widget ui-widget-content ui-
corner-all',
            headerClasses = 'ui-widget-header ui-corner-all',
            messageClasses = 'ui-widget-content ui-state-default ui-
state-highlight ui-corner-all';
```

You'll also notice that the inbox widget we're working on now has a new option – `icons`. The default value of this option is `null`. This new option is passed on to the constructor of each button created by our inbox widget. This is done inside the widget constructor as follows:

```
        this.element
            .find('ul li a')
            .button({icons:this.options.icons})
```

Here, the inbox widget does nothing more than pass the option value forward to the button widget options. So in this sense, inbox is simply a proxy for the button option. Why do we need to do this? We don't have to; user interfaces using the inbox widget could simply set the icon for each button in the inbox widget. However, there are two reasons we don't want to do this:

1. The button widget doesn't support a default icon; the inbox widget could if we wanted it to.

2. If you were to decide you did in fact want a different icon for your inbox widget, it's more convenient to specify this change in the widget constructor, along with any other options. Contrast this with having to build the inbox widget only to specify more options after the fact.

Something else we've changed is the way read and unread messages are displayed. In the previous iteration of our widget, when a user opened a message to read, we added a class to the list item – `inbox-read`. Adding this class to the element didn't actually change anything because there were no style definitions associated with it.

Now, when the inbox widget is first instantiated, we assume that all messages are in an unread state. So opening the message should change the appearance of the list item. We're marking unread messages with the `ui-state-highlight` class so as to call attention to them. When the user opens a message, this class is removed from the item. It then takes the default appearance as illustrated below:

In `jquery.ui.inbox.css`, we've given the inbox widget header more `padding` – 3px to be exact. The header was also pushed a little too far down from the top of the widget. It didn't quite look right. To fix this, we simply removed the top `margin` from the header. Both of these header changes required a new style definition:

```
.ui-inbox h1 {

    margin-top: 0px;
    padding: 3px;

}
```

Also in `jquery.ui.inbox.css`, we've given individual list items more `padding` so they don't look like they're stacked on top of one another.

Finally, in `index.js`, we're passing the folder icon we want to use in each open button for messages.

Have a go hero

At this point, you've seen everything the jQuery UI theming framework has to offer. In this chapter, we've walked through building a custom widget.

Try expanding on our inbox widget by adding new features. Try using a different theme on it or try building your own. Is the widget truly theme-friendly?

Summary

In this final chapter, we've glimpsed inside the jQuery UI machinery to see how they interact with HTML elements at a low level. Essentially, widgets simply attach behavior and visual embellishments to the default appearance of these elements. When a jQuery UI widget is created, the DOM element associated with the widget is modified in some way – a new CSS class from the theme framework is added, and new DOM elements are appended to the structure of the original DOM element. These actions are encapsulated inside the widget, so the developer using the widget doesn't need to worry about additional HTML or classes to basic HTML elements.

We've also seen that custom widgets are implemented the same way as widgets that ship with jQuery UI, the predefined widgets. Custom widgets are also themed in the same way as predefined widgets. Widgets use CSS classes from the theme framework. We've seen classes from this framework all throughout the preceding chapters of this book. Widgets also use CSS classes defined specifically for themselves. These widgets define things like layout, things that are specific to the widget and doesn't apply to a theme.

The inbox widget we've designed and themed has taught us several useful things about designing themes for custom widgets. The first stage is to define the markup that'll be used by developers using your widget. This is an important step. We need to think long and hard in order to make sure that our markup is as simple as possible. The next step is to implement that widget Javascript. The first iteration of this code is usually simplistic. There isn't much for it to do yet aside from find the widget in the DOM and possibly set some potential options. Next, we'll create our CSS specific to the widget. These styles aren't part of the set of theme styles that are applied to other widgets. Finally, we apply CSS classes from the theme framework to our widget. We make it theme-friendly.

That does it for the beginner's guide on building jQuery UI themes. With what you've learned in this book, you should feel confident in creating themes that work in any context. Whether extending something that exists already, or starting from the ground up, you should be able to jump from a jQuery UI theme beginner to a jQuery UI theme expert in no time.

Pop Quiz Answers

Chapter 1

Theme layout

1	a
2	a

Chapter 2

Using jQuery UI

1	a
2	a

Chapter 3

ThemeRoller basics

1	a
2	a
3	a

Chapter 4

The ui-widget class

1	a
2	a
3	a

Chapter 5

The default state

1	a
2	a
3	a

Chapter 6

The highlight state

1	a
2	a
3	a

Chapter 7

Creating theme icons

1	a
2	a
3	a

Chapter 8

Theme corners

1	a
2	a
3	a

Chapter 9

jQuery UI widgets

1	a
2	a
3	a

Index

error message background 152, 153
error message borders 148, 149
error message font 155-157
error tabs border 149-151
Ext JS 44

F

**feedback mechanism, ThemeRoller application
    48**
float property 24
font-family style property 13

G

group selectors 16

H

header borders, ui-widget-header class
    about 92
    border sides 94, 95
    styling 92, 93
headerClasses variable 238
header links, ui-widget-header class 95-97
highlight icons, icon states 178
highlight interaction cue
    background, highlighting 139
    borders, highlighting 136
    button borders, highlighting 138, 139
    date-picker background, highlighting 141, 142
    font, highlighting 142
    message background, highlighting 139-141
    message borders highlighting 136, 137
    message borders, highlighting 137
    message font, highlighting 143, 144
    tabs font, highlighting 144-146
highlight state, interaction cues 135, 136
hover and focus states
    seperating 121, 122
hover icons, icon states 180, 181
hover state, interaction states
    about 118
    hover container selectors 118-120
    hover font styles 123, 124
    hover state font 122
    hover state selectors 118

I

icon states
    about 177
    default icons 177
    error icons 179, 180
    highlight icons 178
    hover icons 180, 181
inbox widget
    basic javascript 223-226
    basic markup 221, 222
    behavior, adding 227-229
    designing 220
    finishing polish, adding 238-243
    goals 223
index.html file 12
interaction cues
    about 133, 134
    disabled state 159
    error state 147
    example, preparing 134, 135
    highlight state 135
    priorities 161
interaction states
    about 99
    active state 126
    default state 101, 102
    example, preparing 100, 101
    hover state 118

J

jQuery
    custom widgets 217
    interaction cues 133
    themes 7
    user interfaces 10
    widgets 9
jQuery environment
    setting up 191, 192
jQuery UI
    CSS framework 25
    CSS, using 38
    dialog options, changing 35
    DOM elements, using 37
    downloaded components, removing 29, 30

W

Widget 218
widget containers
  about 75
  example 76
Widget CSS 218, 219
widget factory 24
widget fonts, ui-widget class
  about 78
  changing 78
  scaling down 79-81
widget form fields, ui-widget class
  about 81
  changing 82-84
widget framework 24
widget icons
  about 167
  default widget icons 167-169
  setting 170, 171

Widget JS 218
widget methods 37
widget options 36
widgets
  about 9
  implementing 220
  relating, to theme 10
  styling 230
  widget structure 9, 10
widget structure 9, 10
widget style
  finishing polish, adding 238-243
  theme CSS 236, 237
  widget CSS 230-235

Thank you for buying
jQuery UI Themes Beginners Guide

About Packt Publishing

Packt, pronounced 'packed', published its first book "*Mastering phpMyAdmin for Effective MySQL Management*" in April 2004 and subsequently continued to specialize in publishing highly focused books on specific technologies and solutions.

Our books and publications share the experiences of your fellow IT professionals in adapting and customizing today's systems, applications, and frameworks. Our solution based books give you the knowledge and power to customize the software and technologies you're using to get the job done. Packt books are more specific and less general than the IT books you have seen in the past. Our unique business model allows us to bring you more focused information, giving you more of what you need to know, and less of what you don't.

Packt is a modern, yet unique publishing company, which focuses on producing quality, cutting-edge books for communities of developers, administrators, and newbies alike. For more information, please visit our website: www.packtpub.com.

About Packt Open Source

In 2010, Packt launched two new brands, Packt Open Source and Packt Enterprise, in order to continue its focus on specialization. This book is part of the Packt Open Source brand, home to books published on software built around Open Source licences, and offering information to anybody from advanced developers to budding web designers. The Open Source brand also runs Packt's Open Source Royalty Scheme, by which Packt gives a royalty to each Open Source project about whose software a book is sold.

Writing for Packt

We welcome all inquiries from people who are interested in authoring. Book proposals should be sent to author@packtpub.com. If your book idea is still at an early stage and you would like to discuss it first before writing a formal book proposal, contact us; one of our commissioning editors will get in touch with you.

We're not just looking for published authors; if you have strong technical skills but no writing experience, our experienced editors can help you develop a writing career, or simply get some additional reward for your expertise.

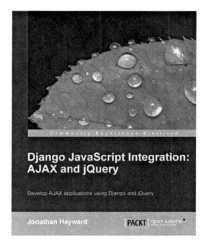

Django JavaScript Integration: AJAX and jQuery

ISBN: 978-1-849510-34-9   Paperback: 324 pages

Develop AJAX applications using Django and jQuery

1. Learn how Django + jQuery = AJAX

2. Integrate your AJAX application with Django on the server side and jQuery on the client side

3. Learn how to handle AJAX requests with jQuery

4. Compare the pros and cons of client-side search with JavaScript and initializing a search on the server side via AJAX

jQuery Mobile First Look

ISBN: 978-1-849515-90-0   Paperback: 216 pages

Discover the endless possibilities offered by jQuery Mobile for rapid Mobile Web Development

1. Easily create your mobile web applications from scratch with jQuery Mobile

2. Learn the important elements of the framework and mobile web development best practices

3. Customize elements and widgets to match your desired style

4. Step-by-step instructions on how to use jQuery Mobile

Please check **www.PacktPub.com** for information on our titles

CPSIA information can be obtained at www.ICGtesting.com
Printed in the USA
BVOW080400110112

280287BV00004B/57/P

jQuery UI Themes
Beginner's Guide

Create new themes for your jQuery site with this
step-by-step guide

Adam Boduch

PUBLISHING

BIRMINGHAM - MUMBAI

jQuery UI Themes
Beginner's Guide

Copyright © 2011 Packt Publishing

First published: July 2011

Production Reference: 1160711

Published by Packt Publishing Ltd.
32 Lincoln Road
Olton
Birmingham, B27 6PA, UK.

ISBN 978-1-849510-44-8

www.packtpub.com

Cover Image by Asher Wishkerman (a.wishkerman@mpic.de)